Structure and Thought in the *Paradiso*

Publication of this book has been made
possible by a grant from the Hull Memorial
Publication Fund of Cornell University

Structure and Thought in the *Paradiso*

By Joseph Anthony Mazzeo

CORNELL UNIVERSITY

CORNELL UNIVERSITY PRESS

Ithaca, New York

© 1958 by Cornell University

CORNELL UNIVERSITY PRESS

First published 1958

PRINTED IN THE UNITED STATES OF AMERICA BY THE
VAIL-BALLOU PRESS, INC., BINGHAMTON, NEW YORK

TO LUCY

Lucia, nimica di ciascun crudele
si mosse, e venne al loco dov'i'era.

Preface

THIS volume grew out of the collection and revision of a series of studies published between 1955 and 1957 in various journals. Although they were all published as independent units, they nevertheless were originally conceived as an interrelated whole. Their focus is on the *Paradiso*, and they are all intended to elucidate the principles of structure and thought which especially govern that part of the poem, though these principles may permeate the whole of Dante's universe as well.

The *Paradiso* as a work of the imagination is basically articulated in terms of medieval neoplatonic doctrines of light and love, light which functions as beauty and love which beauty elicits. From this central perspective, I believe that I have been able to clarify certain problems of Dante criticism concerning the role of Beatrice in the *Comedy*, Dante's view of the meaning of love and beauty in human experience—a view strikingly like Plato's—and his conception of the poet and poetry. Studied in relation to platonic tradition and "experience," elements of the structure and organization of the *Paradiso* become clearer, and this part of the *Comedy* appears as a particular form of "erotic flight" through levels of reality and awareness.

My chapter "Plato's 'Eros' and Dante's 'Amore' " is a direct confrontation of these two great systems of love, and the first, "Dante and the Phaedrus Tradition of Poetic Inspiration," is both an introduction and an example of one way of synthesizing the remaining sections of the book.

Some of my research was supported by a grant from the American Philosophical Society, and I wish to express my gratitude to the society for its aid. I also wish to thank my friends and colleagues who have assisted me in my work at various stages of its progress. Foremost among these are Professor Dino Bigongiari and Professor Marjorie Hope Nicolson of Columbia University. My more recent Cornell colleagues have been especially helpful, and I have profited greatly from the advice of Professor Theodor Ernst Mommsen, Professor Friedrich Solmsen, and Professor James Hutton. All of the above are of course to be absolved from whatever faults this book has.

Those chapters or portions of chapters first published elsewhere and covered by previous copyrights are here reprinted, with some changes, by permission of the original publishers. Chapter I was published as "Dante the Poet of Love: Dante and the Phaedrus Tradition of Poetic Inspiration" in *Proceedings of the American Philosophical Society*, IC (1955), 133–

145; Chapter II as "Dante's Conception of Poetic Expression" in *Romanic Review*, XLVII (1957), 241–258; Chapter III as two articles, "Dante's Conception of Love" in *Journal of the History of Ideas*, XVIII (1957), 147–160, and "The Augustinian Conception of Beauty and Dante's *Convivio*" in *Journal of Aesthetics and Art Criticism*, XV (1957), 435–448; Chapter IV as "Dante and the Pauline Modes of Vision" in *Harvard Theological Review*, L (1957), 275–306; Chapter V as "Plato's 'Eros' and Dante's 'Amore' " in *Traditio*, XII (1956), 315–337; part of Chapter VI as "Dante's Sun Symbolism" in *Italica*, XXXIII (1956), 243–251.

I would also like to thank Cambridge University Press for permission to quote from Thomas Whittaker's *The Neo-Platonists* (1928), J. M. Dent & Co., Ltd., for permission to quote Philip Wicksteed's translation of the *Convivio* (1903), the Harvard University Press for permission to quote from C. S. Singleton's *Dante Studies 1* (1954), John Lane, The Bodley Head, Ltd., for permission to quote from J. D. Sinclair's translation of the *Divine Comedy* (1948), and the Oxford University Press for the use of Paget Toynbee's translation of the *Letters* (1920).

J. A. M.

Cornell University
September 1957

Contents

1

Dante and the Phaedrus Tradition of Poetic Inspiration

THE *Divine Comedy* is, from one point of view, an anatomy of love ending when the traveler, Dante, reaches his goal and becomes one with the "love that moves the sun and other stars." It is also an anatomy of beauty, beauty which takes as many analogous and corresponding forms as there are loves. The universe of the poem is finally entirely reduced in the *Paradiso* to the interplay of love and beauty, beauty which, as will be seen, is primarily manifested *as* light and *through* vision. These two—love and beauty as light—constitute the very structure of the universe and do so functionally: they

1

are not merely architectural elements but the basic concepts in terms of which the poem is articulated and through which it conveys its meaning. They make the journey possible and determine its nature.

Some of the meanings of love, beauty, light, and vision in the work of Dante, especially the *Paradiso,* will be examined to see how important things may be learned about Dante as lover, poet, and pilgrim to eternity. In the course of doing this it will be found that he reconstituted the Phaedrus doctrine of "salvation," love, and poetic inspiration in extraordinary detail. Let it be said right now that it is as certain as these things can be that Dante had no direct knowledge of the *Phaedrus.* On the other hand, if sources are insisted upon, he had no need of the *Phaedrus.* To paraphrase Etienne Gilson, if, in the Middle Ages in Western Europe, Plato was virtually nowhere, platonism was everywhere, in the fathers, in Cicero, in the Arab philosophers, and, indeed, in Aristotle. When Professor Raymond Klibansky and his associates complete their great work of editing the medieval platonic corpus, it will be possible to make a just estimate of the indirect as well as the direct sources of medieval platonism.[1] However, the scattered elements of platonic doctrines of love were everywhere present awaiting a synthesis. The vocabulary awaited a man who had had a platonic experience and had the need and ability to express it. Dante, I think, was just such a man.

Our examination of the *Comedy* begins not with the beginning but the end, for it is there that love, light, and vision have their highest significance, a unique significance which is the key to understanding all the lesser meanings they assume in Dante's imagination. The poem is a voyage of discovery through levels of reality and awareness, and it is the characteristic of such a journey that each successive step forward illuminates understanding of the place just left. Each level of reality both includes and transcends the one below it. Indeed, the lower step only becomes fully intelligible when seen from above.

The *Divine Comedy* closes with the beatific vision, the vision of God's essence. Dante sees what the sense of sight, the physical eyes, could not behold, the goal that reason could not approach, the truth that the intellect could not grasp: the mysteries of the Trinity and the Incarnation, the multiplicity of the material universe integrated into the unity of thought, and the reduction, to transcendent uncreated Being, of the ten categories which exhaust reality.

After seeing the essence of God, Dante's will was transhumanized, raised beyond its mortal and human condition. It ceased to move along the uncertain, fallible, rectilinear path and assumed the eternal, abiding, uniform motion of circularity. This is the motion of heaven, the motion of the angelic intelligences that, attracted by the Holy Spirit, revolve and in their revolutions rotate the sun and the other stars. The Holy Spirit whom Dante finds at the end of his journey is nothing less than Love, the same spirit whose power Dante had felt but had not recognized when it conquered him in his childhood through the beauty of Beatrice. The end of the journey is thus the realization of the meaning of the beginning. The Holy Spirit, Love, is both Alpha and Omega.

The direct vision of the essence of God had been prepared by the vision of the eternal rose whose white petals "rising in more than a thousand tiers" are made up of the hosts of the redeemed and are directly illumined by the light of God. These two main final visions—the eternal rose of the blessed and the direct vision of God's essence—constitute two aspects of mystical contemplation. The first is a vision of the heavenly host bathed in God's light and is therefore imperfect in that it is not yet an immediate experience of God. The second is perfect, immediate, imageless, and inexpressible. So St. Bernard distinguished between the mystical raptures available to less perfect contemplatives who see God *through* Paradise and the perfect contemplatives who experience him directly.[2]

The final visions had been preceded by what is called speculation, from Latin *speculum* or mirror, the approach to God by *reflections* of his essence in mirrors of ever-growing purity and beauty, the theistic ascent of which St. Paul speaks when he says that, although God is invisible, he can be attained by *understanding* the things he has made. The mirrors then are nothing less than all the constituent elements of the created universe, each of which in its manner and degree tells something about God.

Speculation, therefore, is that part of the *Paradiso* which is a progress in time and place and matter, the ethereal matter of the fifth essence which is the stuff that comprises the heavenly bodies and spheres. The journey is, as Dante tells us in the first and fourth cantos of the *Paradiso*, a natural journey; it is under the guidance of Beatrice and extends from Eden through the nine heavenly spheres covering the first twenty-nine cantos of the *Paradiso*. It is a natural journey, however, only in a restricted sense. It is not possible to the sinner but only to the man who, so to speak, has recovered Eden, the man who has understood the horror of sin and who has undergone the purgatorial retraining of the will. To be natural is to be in heart and mind what God intended us to be when he first created us. Only then can we fully see him reflected in his creatures.[3]

The scene of the final progress, the last four cantos of the *Paradiso*, is beyond time and space. This is the goal of mystical contemplation, and it is the eternity of the spiritual and intellectual light of the tenth heaven. The guide is no longer Beatrice but St. Bernard; the journey is no longer in any sense natural, it is not achieved through moral and intellectual effort but through grace alone. The final raptures are therefore gratuitous, bestowed regardless of merit. Dante, *the pilgrim*, nearing the end of his journey knows that if grace is bestowed at all it is granted only to prayer. Therefore *the poet* Dante enclosed the whole moment of mystical contemplation in the chain of prayer going from Beatrice to St. Bernard, from St. Bernard to the Virgin Mary, and from the Virgin to God, at whose direct request the divine essence unfolds itself.

Between speculation and contemplation, between time and eternity, Dante passes over from physical sight to spiritual vision. His sight undergoes utter transformation and he acquires a new sight—he calls it a *novella vista*. Part of the thirtieth canto of the *Paradiso* is devoted to the description of this new sense of sight, one of the most beautiful passages in the whole poem and one of the most original inspiration.

> Io compresi
> me sormontar di sopr'a mia virtute;
> e di novella vista mi raccesi
> tale, che nulla luce è tanto mera,
> che li occhi miei non si fosser difesi
> E vidi lume in forma di rivera
> fulvido di fulgore, intra due rive
> dipinte di mirabil primavera.
> Di tal fiumana uscìan faville vive
> e d'ogni parte si mettìen ne'fiori,
> quasi rubin che oro circunscrive.
> Poi, come inebriate dalli odori,
> riprofondavan sè nel miro gurge;
> e s'una intrava, un'altra n'uscìa fori.

I was conscious of rising beyond my own powers, and such new vision was kindled in me that there is no light so bright my eyes would not have borne it. And I saw light in the form of a river pouring its splendor between two banks painted with a marvellous spring. From that torrent came forth living sparks and they settled on the flowers on either side, like rubies set in gold; then, as if intoxicated with the odors, they plunged again into the wondrous flood, and as one entered another came forth.[4]

This is the heaven of pure light, "light intellectual full of love, love of true good full of joy, joy that surpasses every sweetness."

> Luce intellettüal, piena d'amore;
> amor di vero ben, pien di letizia;
> letizia che trascende ogni dolzore.[5]

The vision of the divine essence, as Dante himself tells us in agreement with the fathers and the doctors of the Church, is not a matter of simple apprehension. It is a *sight of love*, it is an amorous vision. We must recall that God does not simply love, he *is* love. Love is not a quality he possesses, but it is of his very essence. In seeing him we see Love as well as Truth and Goodness. At the moment of the beatific vision, the distinction between will and intellect, the appetitive and apprehensive faculties, sense and thought, disappears. The new sense which has much more vividness than physical sight, much more immediacy than the intellect, and more evidence than reason, sees because it loves and loves because it sees. It is, if we can imagine such a thing, all the human faculties unified and raised to a higher power.

Dante emphasized this amorousness of the beatific vision. Because the Vision of God is the loving sight of a God who is Truth and Beauty and Goodness, Dante was able to preserve the fruit of his years of study and experience as a love poem, as the story of a love engendered by beauty—a beauty which is a reflected light of God—a love, therefore, which because of its ultimate origin in God must rise from material beauty to spiritual beauty and from physical to immaterial light. In his journey, the lover encompasses an understanding of all the modes of love human and divine, loves which are perverse and loves which are holy, loves which are damned forever and loves which have been redeemed, the love which moves the lover and the Love who moves the world.

For in Dante, as in Plato's *Phaedrus*, the love of beauty leads to the same end as the love of wisdom. The *philokalos* as well as the *philosophos* reach the supreme reality which Plato called the plain of truth (*to pedion aletheias*) and which Dante calls God. In Plato, not only do the lover of beauty and the philosopher meet at this exalted point, but they are joined by the lover, pure and simple, and the lover of the arts of the muses, including those poets who are divinely inspired.

For Dante, the spirit of love matures the soul and illumines truth. Thus when, in the sphere of Mercury, Dante is puzzled about the Redemption, Beatrice speaks to him as follows:

This decree, brother, lies buried from the eyes of everyone whose mind is not matured in the flame of love.

> Questo decreto, frate, sta sepulto
> alli occhi di ciascuno il cui ingegno
> nella fiamma d'amor non è adulto.[6]

The same spirit of love engenders poetry, revealing through inspiration and dictation the highest truths which the poet takes down. When in Purgatory he meets one of his predecessors in the art of poetry, Bonagiunta da Lucca, who asks whether he is speaking to the author of the great *canzone* "Ladies that have intelligence of love," Dante replies:

I am one who, when love breathes in me, take note, and in that manner which he dictates within go on to set it forth.

> 'I'mi son un che, quando
> Amor mi spira, noto, e a quel modo
> ch'è ditta dentro vo significando.'[7]

7

This is the secret of Dante's "sweet new style": the true poet is the secretary of the Spirit of Love and Truth in exactly the same sense that the prophets of the Lord were such, for, until Dante, "dictation" was used only to describe the supernatural manner in which the prophets received the truths of revelation. The difference between Dante and his poetic predecessors is the difference between truth and falsehood.

Thus, in Dante as well as in Plato, the poet rises to or has direct and supernatural contact with the absolute source of truth and beauty. But whereas in the *Phaedrus* the poet's ascent is distinguished from that of the lover, in Dante the poet and the lover rise as one. Thus exalted, poetry, that in the learned opinion of Dante's time was contemptuously referred to as a hybrid of degenerate logic fit only for the unschooled, becomes a principal vehicle for the achievement and expression of truth not attainable in any other mode. Far from being a branch of knowledge fit only for the semiliterate, in Dante's hands poetry has become the peer and rival of metaphysics. How daring this claim is can be understood only when we consider the enormous weight of authority, patristic and scholastic, against this view. Much as he once loved Virgil, St. Augustine repeatedly condemns poetry for its untruthfulness and condemns poets as theologians of paganism, regretting the poetic as well as the sensual pleasures of his youth.[8] St. Thomas says that poets are inveterate liars and that poetry is the science which contains the very minimum of truth.[9] The most he will concede to poets is that they make pretty word pictures which it is natural for a man to like.[10] The only proper object of the lies of poets is to inculcate moral virtue in the great mass of people who cannot grasp ideas which are properly stated.

Citations from other authors in other periods could be multiplied indefinitely, but these suffice to give some sense of the prevailing atmosphere in which Dante made his triumphant affirmation of the nobility of the poet and poetry. This revaluation of the art of poetry is of the deepest significance because it came not from any ordinary or even excellent poet, but from a man who was soon recognized as one of the very greatest writers of all time. It is the first and greatest of the revaluations of the various arts which was the permanent conquest of the Renaissance and which modified the extreme and arid rationalism of the time in the direction of a more humane and humanizing culture.

We must now turn our attention to a more precise understanding of the meaning of vision, the light to which it was directed, how this light appeared as beauty, and why it aroused love.

The reader of the works of Dante cannot fail to notice that one strand that runs through and unifies the *Comedy* is the continual repetition of terms of vision and light. From the beginning—"where the sun is silent"—to the end, the *Divine Comedy* is a carefully ordered hierarchy of lights and shadows. Not only are we asked to see clearly but we are asked to see "qualitatively," to distinguish not only degrees of light and vision but kinds of light and vision. It is, as we have seen, in the closing cantos of the *Paradiso* that the degree of light is most intense and that our attention is called to some unique sense of vision. With extraordinary insistence, Dante repeats some form of the verb "to see" every few lines. His insistence would be ridiculous if he were not signifying the divine. With the transition from time to eternity the more sophisticated resources of language are inadequate, and one must revert to a childlike form of emphasis, repetition. His rapture in the possession of his new sight and his intense desire to communicate his joy in the divine vision to his readers make the simplest of rhetorical devices somehow adequate to the expression of the most unimaginable human experience. With mounting intensity, we are brought face to face with that light which is God—the supreme, pure, true, and eternal light. We see him both as *Luce*, the source of light, and as *Lume*, the splendor of this radiated light in the universe of thought. This is the radiance which beatifies and beautifies the angels and the blessed and the light whereby Dante saw the whole universe, "substance and accidents bound together as in one book."

The question for us here is whether the light terms are mere metaphors in the sense that they are pictorial representations of a reality which is capable of being more adequately described in clear, abstract terms or whether they are literally and significantly used. In other words, was Dante one of those, numerous in his time, as well as before and after, who conceived of light as the very stuff of the universe, its principle of continuity extending from physical, material light to a supersensuous, immaterial, supernatural light perceptible only to the eye of the soul?

The question was a familiar one in Dante's time. Modern scholarship calls it the problem of light metaphysics, and its ultimate source is found in Plato. In a striking passage of the sixth book of the *Republic* (507A–509D) Plato tells us that for seeing we need three factors: there may be eyes and there may be colors, but in order that these colors be seen we have need of a third factor—light, the light of the sun. Likewise in knowing we need three factors: there may be a mind, there may be truth to know, but before the truth is grasped we need that light-creating god which Plato calls the Idea of the Good to mediate between the Truth and the Intellect. (Incidentally we might recall here that Beatrice is defined by Dante as one who shall be a light between the truth and the intellect, one of the many indications of her mediatory nature.) The question was raised by both the neoplatonists and the fathers: Is the language here figurative or literal? Some insisted that Plato meant the source of physical light to be a derivative of the source of spiritual light, that he literally calls the sun the offspring of the Good, while others insisted that Plato used the terms analogically and that the language is therefore figurative and suggestive. Whatever Plato meant, both the fathers and the neoplatonists tended to a quite literal interpretation of this passage. For the latter, it was especially useful to take it literally. After all, does not Scripture tell us that God is light and that it is through his light that we shall see light?

St. Augustine obviously accepted some such notion of immaterial light. His doctrine of divine illumination as a substitute for the doctrine of abstraction in the process of understanding implies some such *sui generis* light such as we are here considering.[11]

That the question was much discussed in Dante's time we have ample evidence. St. Thomas, for example, says:

On the question of the existence of a spiritual light there is a difference of opinion among the fathers. Augustine seems to hold that light is more accurately predicated of spiritual rather than corporeal substances while Ambrose and John Damascene maintain that it is only predicated metaphorically of spiritual substances.[12]

As an opponent of Augustine's view St. Thomas cites St. Ambrose (with whom he naturally agrees), respectfully but firmly rejecting the authority of St. Augustine in this matter. The followers of St. Augustine's light metaphysics, according to St. Thomas, are misled by metaphor and figurative language. This is typical of St. Thomas' intense rationalism and distrust of any metaphorical expression. Truth for him is always literal. He allows that certain truths of revelation are so exalted that our finite minds are capable of apprehending them only through indirection, but this is true *only* of revelation. Everywhere else and from any other source, metaphor is a lie.

St. Thomas also cites the anonymous *Liber de intelligentiis,* "On Angelic Intelligences," as advocating the existence of a spiritual light.[13] This book is typical of an extensive literature on light, and its doctrines are very significant for a general understanding of the *Paradiso.* The author of this treatise not only repeatedly affirms that God is literally spiritual light, but also derives physical light from spiritual light. Indeed, light in this work is a veritable Proteus. The entire structure of reality is rendered in terms of kinds of light, material and spiritual light, created and uncreated light, the light of the intellect by which we know and the light of the eyes by which we see. God is uncreated spiritual light, the angels are created spiritual lights, and physical light is the very principle of being. "Let there be light" literally called the universe into existence.

Our anonymous author begins by quoting for authority an Augustinian passage also cited by St. Thomas: "God is light in the literal, not in the metaphorical sense of the term." [14]

Since God is the ultimate source of all existence, he derives from this the corollary that "every substance that exerts any influence on another is either light or possesses the nature of light." [15] He thus reduces all causality and efficaciousness to light.

Light for the author of the *De intelligentiis* has another important property which helps us to understand the amorous journey of the *Paradiso.* It is "the measure of nobility [i.e., beauty and excellence] in that the divine being is communicated to creatures in the form of light so that the more luminous a thing appears, the nobler it is." [16] From this point of departure he concludes that light is the principle of life and that light is the principle of knowledge, the latter because the form of things is light and this same light also makes them intelligible.[17] Form, in the Aristotelian sense, is the principle both of being and of cognition, and in light the form of things is made manifest.

All reality is thus a hierarchy of the multiple kinds and forms of light culminating in the spiritual light which is God.[18] Each higher level of the hierarchy is more noble, causally powerful, vital, as we ascend to the source. Most important for our purposes, *beauty and understanding* also increase as we climb the ladder of light. In this our author echoes many of his famous contemporaries. St. Bonaventura tells us that light is the most beautiful of substances, and for Robert Grosseteste and Thomas of Vercelli, who cite the writings of Pseudo-Dionysius, light is the very principle of beauty itself.[19]

Thus the ladder of light is several things: it is the great chain of being, the ladder of truth and, most important for the student of Dante, *the ladder of beauty*.

The light which constitutes the principle of beauty and knowledge has another important property. Our author tells us:

[Light is] what brings to our apprehensive faculty the highest degree of joy, in that joy always arises from the harmonious unification of a thing with an object which fits or corresponds to this thing; and no relationship can be more harmoniously satisfying than that which binds the light of the soul with the light of the universe.[20]

Thus, light appears as the giver of joy or delectation (*delectatio*), and this joy is nothing less than the subjective aspect of the experience of beauty, *love* in its widest sense. We must recall here that, until the eighteenth century, love and beauty were always correlates. For Dante, the experience of beauty in a work of art is not essentially different from the experience of beauty in a woman, although he was well aware that the latter has its dangers. To admire the beauty of a woman is not the same thing as desiring to possess her. Beauty, wherever and whenever it is found, elicits joyous delectation or love, not lust or possessiveness.

The light of the universe is a hierarchy of luminous beauty, and beauty elicits love in proportion to its intensity. The ladder of light as beauty is thus, subjectively considered, the ladder of love. The eyes, whose function, as we shall see, is to be delighted and lured by luminous beauty, discern beauty in its garment of light whether material or spiritual. Indeed the function of material light as beauty is to lure us upward so that we may understand and love the greater beauty of the spiritual light. Thus Rupertus Tuitens tells us, speaking of the stars:

Visible light has been created in the pattern of spiritual light so that men [attracted by the light of the stars] may thereby rise to it [spiritual light] and increase their understanding of it.[21]

And Dante reminds us frequently that the heavens lure us upward toward God by their beauty.[22]

Let us now examine some of the properties of light in Dante's *Paradiso*. When he passes beyond space and time to the tenth heaven, he sees a ray of immaterial light that materializes itself at a point in the convex surface of the ninth sphere which, as he says, "derives from this ray life and power."[23] This is the same luminous power that communicates being to the entire universe.[24] Dante had *previously* seen this point on the *concave* surface of the ninth sphere.

Impressed with the sight, he did what he had done in the first canto and elsewhere—he quoted literally and with magnificent effect a line from Aristotle's *Metaphysics*. The immense significance of the point of light is best expressed by a short, simple quotation from the man who had *in thought* imagined the place where Dante now *is:* "From that point is suspended heaven and all nature." [25]

Material light is therefore the substantial form of the whole universe, the "light of the universe" which we just encountered as the bringer of joy. It is the stuff which constitutes, unifies, and informs the whole of creation and, as St. Bonaventura elaborates, establishes excellence and dignity in every corporeal thing in the proper degree, giving it power to act and preserving it in its being.[26]

But Dante later sees another point of light, of spiritual light, which connects and unifies the categories of reality in their transcendent, immaterial being. This point is God. This time Dante is filled with even greater awe and joy and he exclaims:

I believe that what I saw was the universal form of this great knot [of categories] for even as I recall it I feel my joy inwardly expanding.[27]

Both these points of light are, so to speak, the centers of the material and immaterial universes, of the universe of sense and the universe of thought, and they are not only filiated but they are in intimate, sympathetic correspondence with one another. Dante reminds us throughout the *Paradiso* that the properties of the physical light of the heavenly bodies directly or indirectly proceed from the immaterial qualities of spiritual light, whether of the angels who move them or of God whose instruments they are.[28]

Everywhere in the *Paradiso* the light of the spheres is also affected and modified by Beatrice and by the spiritual splendor of the blessed souls who appear to welcome Dante. A striking and dramatic instance of this process occurs when Dante and Beatrice enter the sphere of Mercury. Dante says:

Here I saw my lady so joyful when she passed into that heaven's light that the planet turned brighter for it.[29]

One role of light in the *Paradiso* is clear: all substantiality (God, souls, angels, things) and all beauty are reduced to luminosity.

Let us listen now to the soul of Peter Damian for another example of the working of light:

A divine light is focused upon me, piercing through this in which I am embosomed, whose virtue, joined with my own vision, raises me so far above myself that I see the Supreme Essence from which it is drawn. From this comes the gladness with which I am aflame; for to my sight, in the measure of its clearness, I match the clearness of my flame.[30]

A light radiating from the Divinity centers upon Peter Damian and penetrates that light of which he is made. The power of this entering light joined to his sight so *uplifts* him above himself that he is able to see the divine essence from which this light comes. This is the cause of the joyous love with which he burns, and brightness of this burning love is directly proportional to the extent and clarity of his vision.

The state of consciousness of the blessed is here described in terms of what we might call a virtuous circularity. Increase of light results in an increase of love, and the increase of love in turn demands more light and so deeper and deeper into the divine essence.

The spirit of Solomon a little earlier had also described

this same virtuous circularity in the blessed and specifically as the state of the blessed after the resurrection:

As long as the feast of Paradise shall last, so long shall our love radiate this vesture of light. Its brightness corresponds to our love, our love to our vision, and that is in the measure each has of grace beyond his merit. When the flesh, glorified and holy, shall be put on again, our person shall be more acceptable for being all complete, so that the light freely granted to us by the Supreme Goodness shall increase, light which fits us to see Him; from that must vision increase, the love increase that is kindled by it, the radiance increase which comes from that.[31]

This process not only describes the beatified consciousness, but describes the whole process of Dante's ascent. As he passes from sphere to sphere guided by Beatrice, we can see the process at work. Beatrice glows with a greater light and beauty, Dante's love is intensified and, consequent upon his increase of love, he instantaneously and ecstatically is rapt to a higher level of reality. The process begins again at each higher level of the universe, Beatrice luring him up with her increasing luminous beauty which finally becomes so great that only God can fully see it. This pattern is the basic rhythm of the *Paradiso*, describing not only the consciousness of the blessed but the way in which consciousness extends its awareness, increases its understanding. It is the rhythm of Dante's journey through the intelligible world—the universe of thought and understanding—just as his *linear* motion through the spheres represents his journey, *taking place at the same time*, through the sensible world. The circularity is now a spiral: more light, more love which demands still more light, and so from sky to sky, from sphere to sphere, to the infinite Eternal Light.

It is light, spiritual or material, in its role as *beauty*, in its role as the *correlate of love*, which gives us the key to this amorous journey through higher and higher levels of reality and awareness. Let us now turn for a moment to examine what is meant by beauty.

Things are so constituted that a certain bodily aspect reveals directly, if partially, their inner essence, translates their form. This aspect of things is what we call their beauty. It starts a process of knowing which passes from the corporeal to the incorporeal level and from one phase of spiritual beauty to the one higher and purer, up to the source of all beauty and truth.[32]

Correspondingly, man *qua* man is endowed with a sense which enables him to grasp this beauty at its corporeal level and follow its ascent up to the highest. The sense is sight and its organ the eyes.

In classical antiquity, Plato is referred to as the author of this doctrine. In the *Phaedrus* (250D) he tells us that eyesight is not only the clearest but the most clarifying of the senses; it is the sharpest sense whose function it is to grasp corporeal beauty so as to awaken a desire for spiritual beauty.[33]

In the thirteenth century this relationship of the eye to beauty was a commonplace. Eyesight, whose function it is in man to be lured by beauty, is a *knowing sense*, a revealing power or faculty. Hearing serves somewhat the same purpose although not as well, whereas the other senses administer only to the activities that we have in common with the beasts.

That is why to St. Thomas the adjective "beautiful" is reserved for the object of the eyes and secondarily for hearing. We speak of a beautiful picture, of a beautiful landscape, but not of a beautiful piece of bread. The adjective for the other senses is not beautiful but good.[34]

The lure of the beautiful for the eyes is a frequent theme

in Dante, from the first visions and ecstasies of the *Vita nuova* to the final beatific vision of the Trinity. The sight of Beatrice on earth robbed Dante of his senses. All life departed, but the eyes had their vision because love had taken possession of them.[35]

The eyes brought before the beauty of Beatrice on the summit of Purgatory undergo divine ecstatic visions, and throughout the *Paradiso* the great act is that of the eyes as they pursue light and capture beauty.

To the revealing power of beauty Dante has devoted many pages. Beauty, he says, is an external light that makes manifest an internal splendor.[36] A human body is beautiful when the matter of that body is so arranged that it reveals the qualities of the rational and immortal soul. If this is the case, the body will be most beautiful in those parts which are closest to the soul, "balconies" looking in upon the soul. These two parts are the eyes and the lips. The eyes reveal all the inner movements of the soul so that by scanning them we know the soul's acts. But their power is surpassed by the beauty of the smiling lips. For, as Dante tells us, "the smile is a flash of the joy of the soul, a light that manifests outwardly the light that is within." [37]

But the lips are beautiful, they appeal to the eyes, not that this beauty may be felt as with the tactile senses, but rather that they might start a process that begins *in gazing* and ends in the vision of God. This is the message of the great *canzone* "Ladies that have intelligence of love," in the nineteenth chapter of the *Vita nuova*. The eyes initiate love which then fixes on the smile, a smile revealing a beauty so great that it forces the poet's mind up to God. Dante says, "If any one think evil of the poet's praise of the beauty of the mouth of his lady let him remember that it is the smile of this mouth which was his beatitude." [38]

This corporeal beauty awakens love, a love which raises man to God. How does this happen?

Let us turn first to Plato and then see how Dante differs from him. Of all the beautiful things that man's soul saw in that supercelestial plain of truth, only beauty descended to earth and became incarnate. The other glorious things, Justice, Wisdom, Sophrosyne, remained hidden above, perceptible only to the dim uncertain organs of reason. Beauty, on the other hand, was present to be grasped by a sense made expressly for it and for what follows from it, the keen and clarifying sense of sight.

The sight of corporeal beauty awakens the memory of the greater beauty once seen, in the soul's pre-existent state, the incorporeal beauty of the plain of truth which is infinitely greater. In fact, the only purpose of corporeal beauty is to bring about this recollection or *anamnesis*.

Reminded by this beauty once seen, the soul is fired with a nostalgic, irresistible, frenzied yearning to recapture it. This transport is a supernatural obsession. The divine power that possesses the soul is a love which will never give the lover rest until he reaches the plain of truth.

How much of this do we have in Dante? Do we have a clear and final statement that the function of corporeal beauty is to start the soul in its course toward immaterial beauty? Up to God?

This is the first lesson that Beatrice gives Dante on the summit of Purgatory after she accuses him of error:

For a time I sustained him with my countenance. Showing him my youthful eyes I brought him with me, bound on the right way. As soon as I was on the threshold of my second age and changed life [Beatrice died at the end of her twenty-fifth year at the end of "adolescence" and the beginning of "youth"] he took himself from me and gave himself to another. When I had risen from flesh to spirit and beauty and virtue had increased in me I was less dear to him and less welcome and he bent his steps in a way not true, following after false images of good which fulfill no promise; nor did it avail me to gain inspirations for him with which both in dream and in other ways I called him back, so his salvation now came short except to show him the lost people.[39]

When she forces the necessary confession from the lips of Dante following their reunion beyond the grave, she reminds her lover as follows:

Lay aside the sowing of tears and harken; so shalt thou hear how my buried flesh should have directed thee the other way. Never did nature or art set before thee beauty so great as the fair members in which I was enclosed, and they are crumbled in the dust; and if the highest beauty failed thee by my death, what mortal thing should then have drawn thee into desire for it? Truly thou oughtst, at the first shaft of deceptive things, to have risen up after me who was such no longer. No young girl or other vanity of such brief worth should have bent thy wings downward to await more shots. A young chick waits for two or three, but in vain is the net spread or arrow shot in the sight of the full-fledged bird.[40]

She was thus in the body the most beautiful of all created things in either the field of nature or that of art. By the beauty of her youthful eyes she guided Dante along the right course. But bodily beauty is imperfect. When it has reached its maximum, it must pass over into a disembodied beauty, it must reach a level of beauty which is no longer defective, as hers was through being mortal and corruptible. Her death, therefore, was a death of love. The expectation was that Dante would be attracted by the new and greater beauty, that his love would pursue her beyond the grave; but it was not so. He strayed, and only the terrible vision of sin and damnation turned Dante back on the right path, a vision which the beatified Beatrice obtained for him through her intercessory powers.

When, at the close of the erotic flight through the universe, Dante takes his farewell of Beatrice, he utters words in her final laudation which show how well he learned his lesson. It is the moment when her beauty has become so great that only God can see it all.

The enamoured mind that wooes my lady continually burned more than ever to bring back my eyes to her; and if nature or art have made baits to take the eyes so as to possess the mind, in human flesh or in its portraiture, all these together would seem nothing beside the divine delight that shone on me when I turned to her smiling face. And the virtue that her look granted me drew me forth from the fair nest of Leda and thrust me into the swiftest of the heavens.[41]

But how can there be nostalgia in Dante for a beauty once seen and then in part forgotten? He is a Christian and, unlike Plato, cannot accept reincarnation or transmigration of souls.

The answer is that the sight of Plato's plain of truth which each man saw in a disembodied pre-existent state is replaced by that instantaneous contact of the soul with God at the moment of its *creation*.

In one of the most beautiful passages of *Purgatory* he describes how the soul at the moment that it issued from the hands of God experienced a supreme, ineffable happiness and joy. Upon entering the body it became oblivious of this divine happiness except that it constantly carried within itself a vague longing to experience something like what it had once felt. It is the same nostalgia he describes, in *Paradiso* XXXIII, 55 (when he returns from his vision of God), as an *"imprinted passion,"* like that we have upon awakening after a dream which we have forgotten but the joy of which still lingers in us. Driven by desire to experience once again this pleasure, the soul passes from object to object, ever unsatisfied but never discouraged, until with proper guidance it reaches God. It turns to one thing and then another only to find its rest and blessedness in the "true city."

> Esce di mano a lui che la vagheggia
> prima che sia, a guisa di fanciulla
> che piangendo e ridendo pargoleggia,
> l'anima semplicetta che sa nulla,
> salvo che, mossa da lieto fattore,
> volontier torna a ciò che la trastulla
> Di picciol bene in pria sente sapore;
> quivi s'inganna, e dietro ad esso corre,
> se guida o fren non torce suo amore.
> Onde convenne legge per fren porre;
> convenne rege aver che discernesse
> dalla vera città almen la torre.

From his hand who regards it fondly before it is, comes forth like a child that sports, tearful and smiling, the little simple soul that knows nothing, but, moved by a joyful Maker, turns eagerly to what delights it. At first it tastes the savor of a trifling good; it is beguiled there and runs after it, if guide or curb do not divert its love. Therefore there was need for law to be set as a curb; there was need for a king who should at least discern the tower of the true city.[42]

And in the *Convivio* he tells us that having had our origin in God we are impelled to return to him, that our soul, eager for the highest Good at the very beginning of our mortal course, turns to one thing and then another, always expecting to find supreme happiness in each thing. So we see an infant craving an apple and as he grows older yearning for a little bird, and then for beautiful clothing, then a horse, a woman, and finally more and more riches, testing each thing in turn, trying to re-experience its remembered joy but ignorant of when and in whose presence it was first experienced. When the soul comes to know where to look, it is on the road to salvation.[43]

Dante's first experience of love began as an obsession, as a series of crises in which self-control was lost. Over the years, after much disappointment and suffering, error and repentance, through study and prayer, those crises came to reveal themselves as overpowering divine visitations which were only the first stage of the plan of Providence for his salvation as man, lover, and artist. Dante came to see in the irrational crisis not what love is but only the seed of what love may become.

II

Dante's Conception of Poetic Expression

STUDENTS of Dante interested in his views of poetic expression and structure have naturally focused their attention mainly on what he has to say about allegory. He describes both his major work and several of his *canzoni* as allegorical in structure and evidently thought of allegorical theories as providing both an essential description of the nature of poetry and a most important instrument for its interpretation.

Dante discussed allegory in two places: first in the *Convivio* (II, i), before beginning the *Comedy*, and much later, while at work on the *Paradiso*, in the letter to Can Grande della

Scala (7 and 8). Dante's commentators, however, frequently cite or refer to these passages generally, without taking note of the differences between them. Only two attempts, to my knowledge, have been made to explore these differences and arrive at some understanding of their significance: C. S. Singleton's "Dante's Allegory" and Bruno Nardi's studies in *Nel mondo di Dante*.[1]

The problem which arises in confronting these two texts is that, in the *Convivio*, Dante distinguished allegory as used by poets from allegory as understood by theologians, whereas in the letter to Can Grande he referred exclusively to the allegory of theologians as a key to the interpretation of his great poem claiming, in effect, that it is to be read in the same manner as Scripture. In the light of the generally accepted medieval theories of poetic and theological allegory, the difference between these two passages is of great significance. To claim to use the allegory of theologians is to remove the *Divine Comedy* from the category of poetry as his contemporaries understood it.

Although their conclusions are very different, both Nardi and Singleton have made valuable contributions to the solution of this problem. Some of the difficulties they raise, however, can best be solved by placing the study of allegory in the larger context of the problem of metaphor, the *genus*, of which allegory, defined as an extended metaphor, was but a *species*. I would like first to consider these crucial texts in the light of both medieval theories of allegory and modern criticism and then go on to a discussion of Dante's conception of metaphor and its possible relation to the works of Pseudo-Dionysius the Areopagite.

Dante tells us in the *Convivio* that his poems had been misunderstood because they had been read only on the literal and not on the allegorical level. It was therefore incumbent upon

him to explain how his *canzoni* were properly to be read; it
is in this context that he proceeds to discuss allegory:

I say that, as was told in the first chapter, this exposition must be
both literal and allegorical; and that this may be understood it
should be known that writings may be taken and should be expounded chiefly in four senses. The first is called the literal, and
it is the one that extends no further than the letter as it stands;
the second is called the allegorical, and is the one that hides itself
under the mantle of these tales, and is a truth hidden under beauteous fiction. As when Ovid says that Orpheus with his lyre made
wild beasts tame and made trees and rocks approach him; which
would say that the wise man with the instrument of his voice
makes cruel hearts tender and humble; and moveth to his will
such as have [not] the life of science and of art; for they that
have not the rational life are as good as stones. And why this way
of hiding was devised by the sages will be shown in the last
treatise but one. It is true that the theologians take this sense
otherwise than the poets do, but since it is my purpose here to
follow the method of the poets I shall take the allegorical sense
after the use of the poets.

The third sense is called moral, and this is the one that lecturers
should go intently noting throughout the scriptures for their own
behoof and that of their disciples. Thus we may note in the Gos-
pel, when Christ ascended the mountain for the transfiguration,
that of the twelve apostles he took with him but three; wherein
the moral may be understood that in the most secret things we
should have but few companions.

The fourth sense is called the anagogical, that is to say "above
the sense": and this is when a scripture is spiritually expounded
which even in the literal sense, by the very things it signifies,
signifies again some portion of the supernal things of eternal glory;
as may be seen in that song of the prophet which saith that when
the people of Israel came out of Egypt, Judea was made holy and
free. Which although it be manifestly true according to the letter
is none the less true in its spiritual intention; to wit, that when

the soul goeth forth out of sin, it is made holy and free in its power.[2]

In the first paragraph of this passage Dante tells us that all writings, sacred and profane, can be read in four senses and proceeds to discuss the first two of these senses. The first is the literal sense and is simply the primary meaning of the words of the passage as they stand. The second sense is allegorical and is the truth hidden under the "beauteous fiction" of the words as they stand, the literal meaning. Dante then gives an example from Ovid and adds that theologians take the *allegorical* sense in a way that is different from the poets. I wish here to stress that it is only of the allegorical sense that Dante distinguishes between the allegory of poets and that of theologians. Are we then to assume that he thought that the literal sense of Ovid and of Holy Scripture had the same sort of status? Of course not. All that Dante means here, although he does not distinguish it for us, is that the literal sense of any text is what that text apparently says, whether it is literally true, in our modern sense of this term, or figurative.

Part of the difficulty in interpreting medieval discussions of allegory derives from our tendency to define *litteralis* as "literal," when all it means is the sense of a text as such, whether it be a fiction or a literal truth. Dante is not saying that theologians do not take Scripture to be a "beauteous fiction," for this would have been in his view too obvious to mention.[3] He is calling our attention, as Busnelli and Vandelli observe, to an important distinction between the allegorical sense of Scripture and the allegorical sense of a poet like Ovid.[4] The primary meaning of Scripture, whether expressed in plain and literal or in metaphorical terms, conveys truths given to the scribe by direct inspiration of the Holy Spirit. Even when the scribe gives God human attributes, he is not writing allegory but simply using a metaphor to describe a divine attribute. Whatever other senses a passage may have are of secondary intention, superimposed upon the primary meaning whether that primary meaning is a parable, a metaphor, or a historical event.

The poet on the other hand, according to this view, starts with a truth and then proceeds to envelop this truth in a beautiful fiction so that, for him, the allegory is his primary intention, while the literal sense is secondary. The literal sense of Scripture, however, is primary even when the higher senses are "built in," so to speak, and are fully intended.

In the second paragraph of this passage he discusses briefly the third sense, the moral meaning, and refers only to a passage from Scripture. There is no talk of poets at all, and the reference to Ovid is not pursued further, for very good reasons as we shall see. The third paragraph takes up the anagogical sense and again the reference is only to Holy Scripture. In accordance with the standard interpretation of this meaning, Dante points out that the things in Scripture which the words signify may in turn signify other, eternal, things. This is so because God has the power of using both words and things to signify what he wishes to make known. Thus the literal meaning of a passage may, by the realities it signifies, refer through those realities to other realities of an eternal order.

As Bruno Nardi pointed out, Dante's analysis is confused.[5] The medieval grammarians distinguished only two senses in profane writing, the literal and the allegorical. This was the allegory of poets.[6] The theologians distinguished four senses, and it was only Sacred Scripture that could have four senses. Dante does not pursue the example from Ovid through all four levels because according to the teachings of the authorities no profane writer could have all four levels of meaning. The schools distinguished two kinds of allegory, the kind possible to human beings alone and the kind possible to God alone. The former is always made up of words; it is always tied to the *sensus litteralis,* i.e., it conveys its meanings through words whether the narrative these words constitute is literal, in the modern sense, or figurative. The literal sense may also enclose some hidden meaning and this is the allegorical sense, the teaching beneath the veil.

There is a kind of allegory, however, which only God can make: when things or realities (*res*) stand for other things or realities. Any *res* is a *signum* because God made things so that they would also be meanings.[7] Thus we can read the book of creatures and of history. The Bible combines both kinds of "discourse." It, like profane literature, uses words to indicate things, directly or indirectly, i.e., literally or figuratively. But it also uses realities (*res*), things and events, to express other realities of the spiritual and moral order. In the order of verbal expression the Bible has both history and parable, the latter not necessarily historically true but morally true, a pedagogic device for teaching the truth. On the level of signification through things, Scripture describes events and individuals which are types or analogies of spiritual and moral realities. Their significance is not man-made but is "built into" the realities by their Creator. No human writing could have more than the literal sense, the meaning conveyed through the words, and the allegorical sense, the abstract teaching the narrative might enclose. The mystical or spiritual senses do not, strictly speaking, derive from the words or narrative, the *sensus litteralis,* but from the fact that the things and events the words describe are themselves ordered to signify truths of faith in the Christian life or salvation in eternity. This is possible only to God, for only he can order historical events so as to yield a meaning or to refer to a timeless and transcendental reality. Only God can make things and events be signs and speak through nature and history.

The allegory of theologians is strictly a method of interpretation of God's "writing" whereas the allegory of poets is both a method of interpretation and a principle of construction. Man can write and interpret a twofold allegory, whereas only God can write the fourfold allegory of theologians, although man can interpret his "writings" by understanding their principle of construction. In the *Convivio* Dante undoubtedly confused these two allegories. The assumption that both kinds had four senses, the failure to follow through the example from Ovid, his lack of awareness of the metaphysical and theological presuppositions of the anagogical sense, and his generally inconsistent treatment of the question indicate that Dante assumed the structural identity of both kinds of allegory.

Yet in his mature statement of the question Dante simplified and clarified the problem, not by distinguishing more clearly between the allegory of poets and theologians but by suppressing all reference to an allegory of poets. This would imply that Dante believed himself able to confer on things and events those meanings which presumably could come only from God. Neither Dante nor any sane contemporary would have maintained this. On the other hand, it would not be absurd to claim that a man inspired with the spirit of prophecy and poetry could discover the meaning of things and events, could use and manipulate God's language, read God's books and fuse elements therefrom into a book of his own. I believe that Dante was saying something of this kind in the letter to Can Grande, but before discussing the interpretations of this change in his theory of allegory let us consider the passage itself:

For the elucidation, therefore, of what we have to say, it must be understood that the meaning of this work is not of one kind only; rather the work may be described as "polysemous," that is, having several meanings; for the first meaning is that which is conveyed by the letter, and the next is that which is conveyed by what the letter signifies; the former of which is called literal, while the latter is called allegorical, or mystical. And for the better illustration of this method of exposition we may apply it to the following verses: "When Israel went out of Egypt, the house of Jacob from a people of strange language; Judah was his sanctuary, and Israel his dominion." For if we consider the letter alone, the thing signified to us is the going out of the children of Israel from Egypt in the time of Moses; if the allegory, our redemption through Christ is signified; if the moral sense, the conversion of the soul from the sorrow and misery of sin to a state of grace is signified; and if the anagogical, the passing of the sanctified soul from the bondage of the corruption of this world to the liberty of everlasting glory is signified. And although these mystical meanings are called by various names, they may one and all in a general sense be termed allegorical, inasmuch as they are different (*diversi*) from the literal or historical; for the word "allegory" is so called from the Greek *alleon*, which in Latin is *alienum* (strange) or *diversum* (different).

This being understood, it is clear that the subject, with regard to which the alternative meanings are brought into play, must be twofold. And therefore the subject of this work must be considered in the first place from the point of view of the literal meaning, and next from that of the allegorical interpretation. The subject, then, of the whole work, taken in the literal sense only, is the state of souls after death, pure and simple. For on and about that the argument of the whole work turns. If, however, the work be regarded from the allegorical point of view, the subject is man according as by his merits or demerits in the exercise of his free will he is deserving of reward or punishment by justice.[8]

For Bruno Nardi, the statement of allegory in the letter to Can Grande della Scala is also confused. Dante still does not, in Nardi's view, understand the impossibility of any human being's writing an allegory of theologians, and, far from clarifying the question, he compounds his own confusion by assuming that his poem is written in such an allegory. Nardi also observes that what Dante defines as the literal meaning, the state of souls after death, is exactly the same as what he defines as the allegorical meaning, man by his merits and demerits through free choice deserving the reward or punishment of divine justice, for this is precisely what constitutes their state. He concludes that we ought to ignore Dante's claim of using the allegory of theologians.[9]

Nardi, however, does not take account of Dante's *intention* in claiming to use the allegory of theologians, whether or not he understood the careful distinctions of the schools. After all, it frequently happens that to express a new idea or make a new claim one must use an old vocabulary or set it in an old framework. The schema of the schools and many of the distinctions they made strike us as artificial and arbitrary. Modern philosophers of language would not make such a sharp distinction between the plain and the figurative, the literal and the metaphorical, and some of them have defined everyday literal language as nothing but the depository of dead metaphor.

Dante's intention in "misapplying" or "confusing" the linguistic theories of the schools is to call attention to the *truth* of his poem, to remove it from the category of fiction as the grammarians understood that term. If we consider the *Divine Comedy* and the *Vita nuova* as forms of spiritual autobiography, we can understand one possible way in which Dante can claim to use the higher senses which only God can give to men and events. God's providence governed the events of his life as he governed the events of both sacred and secular history. This is true not only for Dante but for everyman. A man looking back over his past may discover what his experiences and actions meant and will discover that some of them—perhaps trivial or unintelligible when they occurred—

will form a meaningful pattern and, taken together, reveal the particular and individual way that universal Wisdom proceeded in its government of the world.

But spiritual autobiography must be distinguished from autobiography in the traditional sense, for it is made up of those events and those alone in which a man can discover the divine intention and meaning. Dante himself tells us that it is improper for a man to speak of himself merely for the sake of doing just that and nothing more. If everything that is and happens has a meaning, it is not for man to know it. Only those events in which there is, and in which he can discern, a higher meaning are fit for disclosure. These are the events which Dante abstracted from the flow of merely empirical autobiography and reset in the framework of a fiction. If, as Nardi holds, Dante confused the two theories of allegory, he did so because neither explained the true status of his poem. It is on the one hand fiction because the journey never happened; it is on the other hand truth because the elements of the poem, cosmological, ethical, and personal, are true. One of Dante's intentions, in discussing allegory, is not so much to advance a theory of explication as to describe a theory of the selection and ordering of significant experience. It is thus that the meaningful intellectual and personal experience of a lifetime is compressed into the "time" of one week. What is truly fiction in the poem is what is necessary to connect significant events and ideas after they have been abstracted from the flow of empirical reality, from the flow of events through time and space.

Charles S. Singleton, in his article on Dante's allegory and in his studies on the underlying structural principles of both the *Vita nuova* and the *Comedy*, has taken seriously Dante's claim of using the allegory of theologians. He maintains that the *Divine Comedy* is written in the allegory of theologians and that, accordingly, it is an allegory of "this and that" not of "this for that." Thus Virgil, a historical figure, has full-blooded existence in the poem; his actions are not fictions designed to convey hidden meanings, but have the status of events. This, therefore, is an allegory of theologians because the literal level is not a fiction in the same way as the story of Orpheus.

Although Dante intended his poem to have, as Mr. Singleton says, "a first meaning which is *in verbis* and another meaning which is *in facto*," [10] this does not quite tell what Dante meant in applying the allegory of theologians to his poem. Let us recall again the sharp distinction between profane or poetic allegory, human discourse in words enclosing an abstract meaning in the narrative they form, and sacred allegory, the spiritual sense of things and events in Scripture as well as the spiritual sense of the discourse of Scripture whether historical or parabolic. These spiritual senses are always of divine origin. In the distinction between the allegory of poets and that of theologians it was not primarily a question of the status of the *sensus litteralis*, of what might be signified *in verbis*. In either allegory this might be figurative and would be subject to the conventional forms of logical and rhetorical analysis.[11] Parts of Scripture such as parables and the Canticles were always interpreted as figurative expressions of religious and moral truths. The real difference hinged on those higher senses in which the realities referred to by the words referred in turn to higher spiritual truths. These higher meanings, the meanings *in facto*, according to the theologians, are precisely what no human being could create. Yet Dante accepted as a principle of construction what could only be a principle of interpretation.

Dante does not claim to create reality; he is saying rather that he can see reality, at least in part, as God sees it. The poet inspired by the Holy Spirit, the Spirit of Love and Truth, receives through the imagination truths which cannot be otherwise known or stated. Of course Dante cannot claim to see all things or to confer on any thing or *res* the status of a *signum*. He can legitimately claim, however, that, by divine inspiration, he has been able to see the God-given transcendental meanings of many of the events of his life and time. If Dante erred in claiming to use the allegory of theologians— and by all the weight of authority he did err—we are a little closer to understanding the nature of his error and why he fell into it. He erred in assuming that the allegory of theologians as understood by the doctors of the Church was a principle of construction like the allegory of poets. He did not realize that the allegory of theologians was, in the view of the interpreters of Sacred Scripture, a principle of construction only for God, not man. On the other hand, he sensed in his own vision of things a penetration, the gift of divine inspiration, which permitted him to see things and events, as God intended them to be seen, with their eternal reference and meaning. Thus, with truth of this order in his poem, it could be read only in some mode analogous to Scripture. Dante may not have understood the allegory of theologians as they wanted it understood, but he saw instinctively that it was this kind of allegory which best described the source and quality of his poem.

Mr. Singleton formulates the underlying presuppositions of Dante's structural imagination when he maintains that the *Divine Comedy*'s structure "imitates" that of reality as the great thinkers of the Middle Ages conceived it. As the universe may be considered the poem of God, so the poem is a kind of microcosm reflecting in its parts the nature of its model:

Allegory and symbolism are both given to this poet, as modes, out of the model which he had ever before him. They are, first of all . . . God's ways of writing. And analogy, in turn, is the comprehensive canon of art by which a medieval Christian poet could do his work as the realist he was.[12]

It is in this sense that the poet may imitate God's ways of writing even though he is, of course, unable to confer on actual things and events any transcendental meanings, i.e., make *signa* out of *res*. Rather, he discovers in things and events the meanings which their Creator gave them. Simply to have imitated God's allegory in any extrinsic way, however, would not have made Dante's allegory anything more than an allegory of poets. What Dante claims is prophetic inspiration and depth of vision, the power to read God's writing in his own experience and to fuse its elements into a coherent whole. His allegory is, in a sense, more than so constructed as to be the image of God's allegory in his book of scripture, where events themselves are seen to point beyond to other events"; [13] it is more than an image because the elements of the poem, cosmological, historical, personal, have those transcendent meanings which God gave and which Dante was able to discover.[14] It is, however, an image in that these elements are set in the matrix of a fiction.

Dante's conception of allegory, however, remains ambiguous. Nardi is undoubtedly right in maintaining that Dante did not understand the allegory of theologians. It is true, at least, that he did not understand it as theologians wanted it understood. It is also true that he uses it to assert the importance of poetry and important conceptions about the nature of poetry and poetic expression. This will emerge more clearly from a consideration of his views on metaphor.

It is in terms of a theory of metaphor, which included allegory, that Dante stated most clearly his views on poetic truth and on the poet's rivalry with the theologian and philosopher in his claim to knowledge of ultimate reality. The most important reference to metaphor in Dante's works is in the letter to Can Grande. This letter, obviously an introduction to the *Paradiso* with general remarks on the nature of the poem and poetry, contains a discussion of the opening lines of the third part. This discussion makes the letter a treatise on light metaphysics as well as a treatise on poetics. The fusion of poetics and light metaphysics is necessary not simply because of the imagery and conceptions in the lines on which Dante comments; it is necessary also because Dante treats metaphor in terms of light metaphysics.

Light metaphysics reduced all substantiality—God, souls, angels, things, the human intellect—to forms of light, uncreated and created, material and spiritual, sensible and intellectual. It reduced the hierarchies of being, truth, beauty, perfection—indeed of all "value"—to a hierarchy of light ascending to the very Primal Light itself, spiritual, uncreated, divine, the vision of which is the vision of all. This vision, even though Dante was not Aeneas or Paul, was yet given to him; but he cannot express it in its fullness, both because it is above the power of language to express and because he cannot recall all of it. Citing the authority of St. Paul, St. Augustine, St. Bernard, and Richard of St. Victor in his claim to direct vision of the highest reality,[15] he goes on to explain why language is inadequate for rendering the vision in its fullness:

He saw, then, as he says, certain things "which he who returns has neither knowledge nor power to relate." Now it must be carefully noted that he says "has neither knowledge nor power" —knowledge he has not, because he has forgotten; power he has not, because even if he remembers, and retains it thereafter, nevertheless speech fails him. For we perceive many things by the intellect for which language has no terms—a fact which Plato indicates plainly enough in his books by his employment of metaphors; for he perceived many things by the light of the intellect which his everyday language was inadequate to express.[16]

In this passage poetic theory and light metaphysics are linked and metaphor is revaluated. In the doctrine of the schools poetic metaphor merely adorned and even obscured the truth, while theological metaphor, as found in Scripture, was the only way of expressing truths beyond human comprehension.[17] In citing the use of metaphor by Plato, a philosopher, Dante emphasizes that to express the ultimate reality, in itself inexpressible, even the thinker must resort to techniques which prevailing doctrine considered chiefly the property of poets. The poet-seer who journeys along the ladder of light to the Primal Light arrives at truths which only metaphor and allegory—the latter simply an extended metaphor—can express. In this way the poet is the rival and peer of the thinker. The Holy Spirit, in dictating Scripture to its divinely inspired scribes, had, so to speak, used metaphors to accommodate supraterrestrial truths to terrestrial intellects. So, too, the poet and thinker both may reach a realm of vision or thought, the content of which, when they "return," can be conveyed only symbolically. The implication is clear that there may be a plurality of symbolic and metaphorical expressions of those ineffable things which can be seen by the light of the intellect. Plato, after all, was no Christian, and what he saw by the light of the intellect was not enough to keep him out of Limbo. But even certain truths of the natural or philosophical order are not to be stated literally.

The allusion to Plato is even more striking when compared to what St. Thomas has to say about him and his use of metaphor. In the commentary on the *De anima* of Aristotle, St. Thomas takes up the question of Aristotle's refutation of

Plato, trying to extenuate Aristotle for criticizing Plato and, at the same time, justifying the former's criticism. He points out that, often, Aristotle criticizes not what Plato actually meant but the apparent meaning of his words. Aristotle had to do this because Plato's method of teaching was defective; for he constantly used symbols and figures of speech, as when he called the soul a circle, thereby obscuring by a figurative meaning his actual literal meaning. St. Thomas adds that when Plato called the soul a circle, he was speaking only metaphorically and did not mean that the soul was anything quantitative or circular, but—as St. Thomas repeats—lest there be any error Aristotle argues against the literal interpretation of the words.[18] Contrary to the view in the letter to Can Grande, Plato uses metaphor as a pedagogical device—and a bad one it is for St. Thomas—not, as Dante infers, because what he has to say cannot be said in any other way.

St. Thomas also comments on Orpheus' erroneous opinion about the soul. He is coupled with Musaeus and Linus as a primitive poet-theologian who wrote in verse about philosophy and God. He was in error, immersed in the fictions of the imagination, but his eloquence helped civilize wild and bestial folk. St. Thomas would thus say that eloquence—metaphor, image, simile—may have a civilizing function, but he obviously agrees with Aristotle on the inadequacy of the poet-theologian.[19]

For Dante, however, poetry like philosophy gives truth. The poetry of a Christian who writes what Love or the Holy Spirit dictates gives Christian truth. A man, in a moment of mystic rapture, may have an inexpressible vision for which he must find some adequate expression. The Christian poet imitates the prophet inspired by God in accommodating a vision of saving truth to his readers "to remove those living in this life from a state of misery, and to bring them to a state of happiness." Thus, the branch of philosophy to which the *Comedy* is subject, "in the whole as in part, is that of morals or ethics; inasmuch as the whole as well as the part was conceived, not for speculation, but with a practical object." [20]

The metaphors of the Holy Spirit are those which God chose to express his truth, accommodating himself to a human comprehension in order to lead it to the pure truth. The seer and philosopher, granted a vision of the truth, must do likewise. Evidently, theological metaphor does not exhaust the meanings of the divine light that men can ascertain. Dante claims a personal revelation that is intensely individual and, at the same time, universal, for it is dictated by Love or the Holy Spirit itself. The expression of this vision is a poem whose purpose, like that of Scripture, is to lead men to salvation. The poet is thus a prophet, expressing what he receives by divine inspiration. A true poem is nothing less than a supplement to Scripture. [21]

Theology, the light of revelation, must use metaphor to express that light; poetry and philosophy, expressions of the light of the intellect, also must use metaphor to express their light. All modes of discourse, in their various ways, constitute converging paths to the Primal Light itself. Poet, philosopher, theologian, prophet, and true lover meet on the road to the Absolute.

Thus both poetry and philosophy use metaphor to express truths which would be otherwise inexpressible. There is a considerable difference between this view and the conception in the *Convivio* of poetic metaphor as a beautiful lie embellishing a truth, sweetening some abstract moral idea. Between the *Convivio* and the letter to Can Grande, Dante had come to see that the fables of poets, their imaginative narratives, could have more than one kind of relationship to truth.

The fiction of the supernatural journey in the *Comedy* is not a fiction in the same sense as the fictions about Orpheus, for example, in pagan poetry. It is rather what we would call a platonic myth, a rendering in terms of time and space of the intuition of eternity. Time, as Plato said, is the moving image of eternity, but because it is a *moving* image, it is to some extent fictitious. Yet it is an image, a representation of an otherwise inexpressible reality. The visions which enter the imagination directly, without the medium of the senses, may have behind them the authority that lies behind the visions of Holy Writ. Love dictates them as it dictated to the prophets of old, and the poet must render what the intellectual or divine light, formed in heaven, "either of itself or by a will which directs it downwards," gives it.[22] The *Paradiso* and indeed the whole of the *Divine Comedy* is a translation into terms of sensible light of a timeless vision of a spiritual or intellectual light; an adaptation for physical eyes of what was seen by the eyes of the soul.

Others before Dante had observed that Plato used metaphor and allegory to talk about philosophy, among them St. Thomas, who felt that such a figurative use of language was bad pedagogy. We find a more typical reaction to philosophic metaphor, however, in Abelard's *Introduction to Theology* where he says that Plato used figurative terms such as *anima mundi* and *zoön* in the *Timaeus* to hide philosophic truth from the vulgar.[23] Yet this too is a negative, nonfunctional conception of metaphor.

The conception of metaphor and allegory in Dante's later works bears closest resemblance to some of the ideas of Pseudo-Dionysius, who had a profound effect on Dante and who may be a source in this matter. Dionysius distinguished two methods, *equally allegorical*, philosophical and theological, for coming to some knowledge of an ultimate reality which is beyond all predication.[24] These two methods actually constitute two theologies. One seeks to achieve clarity; its proper domain is the visible, and it proceeds by demonstration. The other presupposes an initiation. It proceeds by symbols, and its proper domain is the *unutterable*.[25] Symbolism is a result of the necessary diffraction of the invisible spiritual light through an imperfectly transparent medium. Thus philosophical and scriptural modes of symbolism are closely related. One and the other use words to designate one single reality, in itself inexpressible and including in itself, at the same time, both affirmation and negation. For Dionysius only paradoxical terms can be used to describe the luminous and the more than luminous darkness, which terms both *hide* and *reveal* the divine mysteries.[26]

The Light which diffracts itself through an imperfect medium and creates symbols of itself is also Beauty and Good, while Love is the stimulus which drives every being through images toward perfect Beauty. In God, this love is the source of an infinite outpouring which leads him to create the symbolic universe. Love also leads to ecstasies because it takes lovers out of themselves and transports them to higher realms. It makes superiors in the celestial and ecclesiastical hierarchies guide inferiors, it unites equals and makes inferiors strive to unite themselves with those orders above them which share more in the divine love.[27]

It is clear how, with some modification, reading "poet and philosopher" for philosopher and "poet-lover" for lover, we find here much of Dante's conception of the lover-poet and the value of poetry. All he had to do was affirm that all forms of discourse, poetic and philosophical, are equally metaphorical when it comes to the expression of eternity. The distinction between what the words convey and the allegorical meanings of the things they designate is, of course, still valid within this larger context. But what the words convey is in either case figurative and metaphorical because they refer to a timeless reality which cannot be apprehended directly or "literally."

In a striking passage of Epistle IX, Dionysius points out that those who have perceived theological doctrine clearly, without a veil, make for themselves some figure which aids them to *understand* what they have perceived.[28] The *Comedy* is offered to us, I believe, as just such a "figure," the result of vision in search of understanding.

A figure is of course a sensible image, and Dionysius persistently maintains that figures not only help us understand what we have grasped of spiritual reality directly, but lead us to that reality.[29] The light which the sacred hierarchy imparts to the initiated and which leads them to immortality also diffracts into an imperfectly transparent medium creating symbols and figures of itself.[30] These symbols either help us to understand what we have already seen or lead us to an understanding of what we have never seen before and to a luminous, painless immortality.[31]

This view of allegory is very different from that of the schools of Dante's time, where literal and figurative expression, philosophical and theological allegory, were sharply distinguished and truth was considered the exclusive prerogative of literal statement. Dionysius studies allegory as part of the problem of metaphor and symbolism. As in the letter to Can Grande, all these questions of expression are answered ultimately in terms of light metaphysics. We know that, between the writing of the *Convivio* and the letter to Can Grande, Dante had studied Dionysius. Since the particular blending of light metaphysics, poetic theory, and theology in the letter is paralleled only by Dionysius, it would seem that his conceptions of linguistic expression as rendering a luminous, imageless reality helped Dante solve the problem of the nature of poetic expression.

Thus Dante puts poetic discourse or allegory, as given to a prophetically inspired Christian poet, on a par with the allegory of theologians, for they have the same source. Poetic allegory is on a par with all other forms of human discourse and is equal to the highest, because in relation to what the Truth is in itself, no discourse is fully adequate. What love dictates to the poet and prophet, what the illuminated intellect of a philosopher or theologian can see, is more than language can express without recourse to metaphor and indirection.

In proclaiming his allegory equal to that of the theologians, Dante did not use the careful and precise analyses of the schools; he reformulated the question, after Dionysius, as the problem of metaphor and indirection in human expression of ultimate truth.

If Dante used things and events to signify spiritual and moral realities, it is because God gave them their significance. He merely *discovered*—through study and through dictation by the Holy Spirit—the God-created meaning of Beatrice, of the events of his life. He *learned* the meanings that God gave to natural objects like the sun when he created them. All that he learned about the significance of things he worked into his poem. The journey is a "literal" one—*litteralis* in the strictly medieval sense because the words describe a journey. It is, on the other hand, metaphorical in that the figurative journey renders an otherwise inexpressible vision. Dante, the poet, rivals the theologian because he has been able to discover God's meaning in things and events. He was able to do this by study and by the grace of Love. He rivals the philosopher because he had a vision of the truth by the light of the intellect which he, like the philosopher, could express only through metaphor. He rivals the prophet because the Holy Spirit, the flame of love, inspired him and dictated to him its truth.

Dante's mature thought on the question of metaphorical expression, *eo nomine,* besides the important references in the letter to Can Grande, is found in the well-known passage in *Paradiso* in which he discusses the theory of accommodative metaphor to explain how the elect appear in the spheres while they "really" are in the empyrean:

These have shown themselves here, not that this sphere is allotted to them, but in sign of the heavenly rank that is least exalted. It is necessary to speak thus to your faculty, since only from sense perception does it grasp that which it then makes fit for the intellect. For this reason Scripture condescends to your capacity and attributes hands and feet to God, having another meaning, and Holy Church represents to you with human aspect Gabriel and Michael and the other who made Tobit whole again. What Timaeus argues about the souls is not like that which we see here; for what he says he seems to hold for truth. He says that the soul returns to its own star, from which he believes it to have been separated when nature gave it for a form; but perhaps his view is other than his words express and may have a meaning not to be despised. If he means the return to these wheels of the honour and the blame of their influence, his bow perhaps strikes on a certain truth. This principle, ill-understood, once misled almost the whole world, so that it went astray, naming them Jupiter and Mercury and Mars.[32]

Referring to the theory of accommodation in biblical metaphor and in Plato's *Timaeus,* Dante here explains how and why the blessed simply appear or manifest themselves in the planetary spheres; but he tells us at the same time that this is what he is doing in his poem. Dante, the character in the poem, is told that, although they are really elsewhere, the blessed appear to him in this way because he must have sensuous images to discern truth. The wayfarer has not yet acquired the new faculty which will permit the direct intuition of reality. At the same time Dante, the poet writing the poem, is telling how to understand the nature of his metaphor and refers—this is most important and daring—to metaphor in Scripture and in Plato. As in the letter to Can Grande, he affirms that he has seen things by the light of the intellect which can only be described to us, if at all—for Dante the poet is writing as one of us, a man once more in a natural condition—through metaphor, indirection, and myth. The "vostro ingegno" of line 40 is a plural and refers to us all. We must recall, however, that Dante finally does see ultimate realities without anthropomorphic traits and that he sees the angels both in human shape and as luminous forms. In the theory of accommodative metaphor as applied to Scripture, representations of divine things were deliberately crude so that they might reach even the simplest of men. It was the duty of the more intelligent to refine these images to find the truth they contained. Not all images of divinity, however, could be so conceptualized, for some truths were too high for the human intellect to render abstractly.

Thus, in this passage, Dante is at a lower level of consciousness, a level at which he is capable of penetrating the philosophical use of metaphor in the *Timaeus*, but not yet, as pilgrim, capable of seeing the blessed as they are. He finally sees them not only as they are but as they will be after the resurrection, in the possession of their glorified bodies. The images of the realities of the *Comedy* gradually correct themselves. The souls of the blessed beginning with the sphere of Mercury after it increases in light are hidden in their own light and are finally seen in an eternal present in which they are as they will be.

The angels in *Inferno* and *Purgatorio* appear in human

form; later, however, others appear as circles of light revolving around God seen as a point of infinite intensity and minuteness. But the divine mind—the point of light—is also the "place" of the *primum mobile* and "encloses" in its "immensity" the whole of the corporeal universe. The angels, the movers of the spheres, are also seen in two orders of arrangement. As circles of light, the highest rank of angels is manifested as the innermost one, the nearest to the central point of light which is God. As movers of the spheres, they are described so that the highest mover is the outermost from the center which is the earth. "Thus, by symbol, it is finally suggested that immaterial essence is beyond distinction of the great and small in magnitude; but even at the end the symbolism has not disappeared." [33]

There is another, more rapid and varied sequence of images which Dante experiences upon his acquisition of a new sense of sight. In *Paradiso* XXX the first image is of a river of light, then the souls appear as beautiful flowers on the banks of the river with angels as sparks flitting about like bees. The river next becomes a sea of light and banks or tiers rise up around it—the elect as they will appear in their glorified bodies—and we see the rose whose "yellow" is the floor of the "arena," the sea of light, while the rose itself is white (*Par.* XXXI, 1).

The rose in turn undergoes transformations. It becomes successively a garden, a kingdom, an empire. As a flower it has two roots; but it also has a stairway and keys. This whole sequence of imagery is a series of accommodations to a reality which the individual images both hide and disclose. So as Dante penetrates more and more deeply into the "lofty light which in itself is true" (*Par.* XXIII, 54: "dell'alta luce che da sè è vera"), it is only the appearance of the immutable and simple Light that changes as Dante's vision gains in power:

Now my speech will come more short even of what I remember than an infant's who yet bathes his tongue at the breast. Not that the living light at which I gazed had more than a single aspect—for it is ever the same as it was before—but by my sight gaining strength as I looked, the one sole appearance, I myself changing, was, for me, transformed.[34]

Thus Dante assimilates objects of thought to objects of sense, the sequence of symbolic representation of a particular reality bringing us closer and closer to what that reality is in itself. The progression of images is not only linear and sequential, each successive one a closer approximation of reality, but in portraying those immaterial realities which are the essence of paradise, one can go only so far when he finds his path cut off: "And so, picturing Paradise, the sacred poem must make a leap like one that finds his path cut off." [35]

A leap to what? To another set of images, to another part of the landscape which he is trying to describe, to another aspect of that level of reality where the poet finds himself which is capable of being imaged.

III

Dante's Conception of Love and Beauty

LOVE in the Aristotelian tradition of the schools was conceived as the natural inclination of anything whatsoever toward its object. This inclination was found to operate in different objects in different ways: in an intellectual nature it is a function of the will, in sensible natures it is a function of the sensitive appetite, and in natures devoid of any cognition it is a function of the nature being ordered to some end.[1]

This doctrine in the course of its development had come to be related in various ways to the complementary Aristotelian theory of weight as due to natural place. Strictly speaking, only corporeal objects lacking in cognition had a natural place to which they tended, and in their case alone was appetition equivalent to weight or gravity. St. Thomas, for example, is careful to point out that it is ridiculous to attribute natural place to spiritual substances except by analogy.[2]

On the other hand, the notion of natural place was extended to the spiritual realm so that appetition or love became simply the desire of all things, corporeal and spiritual, to attain the "place" in the universe, material or immaterial, that was proper or "natural" to them. Thus as air and fire go up and earth and water naturally go down, so all things seek their place and man seeks his "true place" in heaven. It is in this form, not in the more properly Aristotelian form, that St. Thomas expounds, that we find the doctrine of love as a cosmic principle in Dante; his "spiritual gravity" is the correspondence between states of soul and their proper or natural place in the universe. The equation love equals weight, *amor* equals *pondus*, so basic to the moral and physical cosmology of Dante's poem, was no mere similitude to him or to St. Augustine, who may have been a source for Dante in this matter. After pointing out the manner in which all the orders of reality seek their own good or their own place in the order of things, St. Augustine affirms that weight is to body what love is to soul.[3] Even more explicitly, in a moving passage of the *Confessions*, St. Augustine compares the soul's desire for rest in God with the manner in which all bodies seek rest in their natural place in the universe.[4]

Boethius, in the *Consolation of Philosophy*, echoes this Augustinian conception and sings a song of praise to God who creates souls and, scattering them throughout the universe, afterwards calls them back to himself, their Good and Origin. They return to him as fire returns to its natural place.[5] In Book III Boethius points out that each thing must find its own proper course again and rejoices in its return to its own place. Nothing can retain that order with which it is endowed unless in some way it unites its rising (*ortum*) with its end (*finis*) and so makes immutable its own circular course.[6] Thus the theory of love as a generalization of the doctrine of natural place appears as a process of outgoing and return. Man loves and desires because his home is heaven. In Plato and the neoplatonists, the doctrine of "return" was associated with the pre-existence of the human soul. For orthodox Christians such as Boethius and St. Augustine, the soul did not pre-exist, but it "returns" to God as to its Creator.

In the thirteenth century the author of the *De intelligentiis* echoes this Augustinian equation of *amor* and *pondus*. The natural place of a nature is where it comes to rest. What lightness and heaviness are to corporeal substances, love and fear are to spiritual substances, for love "elevates" and fear "depresses." [7]

Thus, for the Christian, the neoplatonic doctrine of return to the One is modified to free it from its emanationistic and pantheistic consequences. The soul "returns" to God because it came from a God who created it, not because it literally returns to a supernatural world in which it pre-existed. It desires to return because of the *nisus* which God implants in all created things, a *nisus* which is not so much a yearning for a pre-existent state based on reminiscence of the bliss of that state, as a divinely implanted tendency to return to the Creator in whose "presence" the soul was formed in the very moment of its creation.

In the *Convivio* Dante discourses at great length on love and defines it as nothing other than the spiritual union of the soul and the beloved object, a union the soul seeks by nature.

If it is free it achieves this union sooner than if impeded, but the natural impulse is always present. Dante explains, citing the authority of the *Liber de causis*, that this natural impulse is present in the soul because it is created by God, and, as an effect of the First Cause, it partakes of the nature of that cause to the extent that it is able and according to its own proper nature. Every form partakes of the divine nature not in the sense that the divine nature is divided, but in the same way that the other heavenly bodies partake of the nature of the sun. The nobler forms share to a greater degree in the divine nature, and the human soul, since it is the noblest of all the forms generated beneath the heavens, receives most of the divine nature.

Since the first cause is being, the source of existence, it is natural for anything to want to exist in God. The human soul desires with all its power to be, and because its being depends on and is preserved by God, it desires by nature to be united to him in order to strengthen that being. Since God manifests himself in different degrees in his creatures and the human soul naturally desires union with God, it seeks to unite itself spiritually more strongly and quickly with an object the more perfect that object appears to it to be. This "appearance" depends on whether the judgment (*conoscenza*) is clear or impeded, and this union is love, the union of a soul with something else which fits that thing. It is what the soul finds fitting as an object of love which reveals what is within the soul, its state and quality. By discerning what the soul loves in the world without, we discover what is within. The lady in whom so much of the divine light was revealed was the object of this kind of love.[8]

Every level in the order of creation has its own kind of love or desire. Simple bodies have a natural love for their own proper place. Thus earth always tends downwards to the center, and fire has a natural love to ascend to the circumference adjoining the heaven of the moon. The primary composite bodies, such as minerals, have a natural love for that place which is suitable for their generation. Such is the place in which they grow and acquire vigor and power. Plants, which are the first of all creatures endowed with soul, i.e., the vegetative functions, more obviously manifest this love. They display a preference to grow in places adapted to the requirements of their natures, e.g., some plants grow well by water, others at the foot of mountains, and if they are transplanted they either die or love, so to speak, sadly, like separated lovers. Animals not only more obviously love their own particular place but love one another; man, possessing a portion of the nature of every one of these lower creatures, can and does experience all these kinds of love as well as his own specific love for all perfect and noble things, a kind of love he possesses by being the noblest of created things under the heavens.[9]

It is because he possesses love of the first kind, that of simple bodies, that man "loves" to sink downwards and is fatigued if he goes against this tendency, or upwards. By reason of the nature of mixed body he loves the season of the year and the place wherein he was generated. Hence everyone feels best physically when he is in the place of his birth and at the time of year in which he was generated. By possession of the vegetative nature or soul, man has a natural desire and affinity for certain foods which will help to make him strong. This kind of desire for food is to be carefully distinguished from the kind arising from sensuous appetite, by which a man might eat foods that are bad for him. It is the animal soul in man, i.e., the sensitive soul or the unity of the faculties of sensation, which makes man feel desire following upon sensible apprehension. This is the love most in need of control because its activity is excessive, especially in regard to the pleasures of touch and taste.

The last faculty, the truly human or even angelic nature, is the rational soul by which man has a natural desire for truth and virtue. From this "affection" derives true and perfect friendship of the kind that Aristotle described in the eighth book of the *Ethics*. This nature is the mind, and Dante adds that when he spoke of love discoursing to him in his mind he meant this kind of love for truth and virtue, the love springing from the noblest nature. He says this in order that no one might hold the false opinion that he was referring to the delights of sense. When in the poem on which he is commenting he says "desiringly," he means to call attention to the intensity and continuing duration of this love. It was so powerful, it so stirred his mind, that his intellect went awry. In thinking about his lady he wished to demonstrate things about her which he found himself unable to understand, and he was often so wrapped in thought and bewildered about her that his outward appearance was of a man out of his mind (*alienato*).[10]

It is important here to observe that the contemplation of the beauty of the lady led him to the perception of truths about her which he could not understand. The effort to understand so dominated him that he seemed as one outside of himself. This "alienation" is nothing else than the description of the "madness" of ecstasy or rapture, a rapture which involves the intuition of truth not fully understood.

So far there are only two differences between the scale of love expounded by Dante and the common Aristotelian doctrine of the schools typified by St. Thomas. First, in applying the doctrine of natural place, Dante does not attempt to distinguish between corporeal and spiritual substances. The equation of gravity (*pondus*) and love (*amor*) is carried right through the whole scale of creatures. Secondly, Dante places special emphasis on the fact that man is a microcosm of all these loves; as we shall see, Dante makes fruitful use of this idea and closes his discussion by describing the effect of the beauty of the "lady" in terms of rapture, madness, or ecstasy.

The most important difference between Dante and the doctrines of the schools is that the union of loves in man is dynamically and not statically conceived. Dante accepted the commonplace that the human soul possessed all the faculties of the lower souls, but he set these souls and their "loves" in a dialectical motion. An objective ladder of "goods" or objects of love corresponds to this ladder of desires, and desire restlessly pursues Absolute Good and Beauty through a hierarchy of objects. The soul has its origin in God and is impelled to return to him. It is eager for the Highest Good at the very beginning of its mortal course, a course which it never traveled before. It is like the pilgrim who travels along an unknown road and believes that each house he sees ahead is the inn he is looking for; disappointed in each one in turn, he puts his faith in the one farther on until he finds the right one. The soul similarly directs its eyes toward the goal of the Supreme Good, but is not fully aware of this and therefore often mistakes a lesser good for its goal. Because the pilgrim soul has little knowledge and experience, it magnifies things of little value and first of all begins by desiring such things. So it turns to one beautiful thing after another, always expecting to achieve supreme joy and always disappointed.[11]

Elsewhere in the *Convivio* (IV, xxiii, 3; IV, xxviii, 2) Dante refers to this natural desire to return to God as a return to the most high and glorious sower of nobility or a return to the port from which the soul set out on the journey over the sea of this life. The gift of nobleness finally returns to safe harbor in God, together with that most noble part of the soul which cannot die.

In the *Purgatorio* (XVI) he develops this doctrine of a natural desire in man to return to God more explicitly and with an interesting and significant addition. The restless dialectical movement up the ladder of love is a true eros, for the soul fixes its eyes on the Supreme Good, without being fully aware that it is doing so. Its restless yearning is compounded of unconscious knowledge and what we might call "conscious ignorance," the true platonic love nostalgia, the yearning for a beauty once seen and then in part forgotten. Plato, as we have seen, explained this state as the result of a "fall" from a pre-existent state in which the disembodied soul saw the plain of truth. In Dante the sight of the plain of truth is replaced by the instantaneous joyful contact of the soul with God at the moment of its creation.

The state of "forgetfulness," which Dante describes as the state of every human being when it enters this world, is actually the same state that the mystic has after he has descended from his instantaneous and brief contact with God. He experiences a failure of intellectual and visual memory, but the joy of the experience lingers.

From that moment my vision was greater than our speech, which fails at such a sight, and memory too fails at such excess. Like him that sees in a dream and after the dream the passion wrought by it remains and the rest returns not to his mind, such am I; for my vision almost wholly fades, and still there drops within my heart the sweetness that was born of it.[12]

It is thus, Dante continues, that the snow loses its stamp when it is melted by the rays of the sun and the Sibyl's utterances were lost when the leaves on which they were written were scattered by the wind.

> Così la neve al sol si disigilla;
> così al vento nelle foglie levi
> si perdea la sentenza di Sibilla.

Thus the *Paradiso* points back and clarifies the past journey. The state he describes here is not as "unknowing" as the state of ordinary human beings, for Dante has had a second contact with God given to few men. He thus has "forgotten," but he can identify the source of his indwelling joy. He can no longer mistake a lesser good for the Supreme Good which alone can satisfy the desire to re-experience that joy.

Shortly afterward, in the final canto, he calls our attention again to this same state when he identifies what he saw, not by calling it to mind—that is impossible—but by "recollecting" and re-experiencing the joy and happiness which attended the vision. He *believes* he saw the transcendent unity of substance and accidents because his joy expands. Yet the experience as *comprehended*, as *immediate*, went into a deeper oblivion than that which twenty-five centuries cast on the exploits of Jason:

I think I saw the universal form of this complex, because in telling of it I feel my joy expand. A single moment makes for me deeper oblivion than twenty-five centuries upon the enterprise that made Neptune wonder at the shadow of the Argo.[13]

Similarly, in *Par.* XXIII, after Christ appears to him, Dante has a rapture, and he cannot recall what became of his mind. He hears the voice of Beatrice in a state similar to that of one trying to recall a forgotten dream:

As fire breaks from a cloud, swelling till it has not room there, and against its nature falls to the earth, so my mind, grown greater at that feast, was transported from itself and of what it became has no remembrance.

"Open thine eyes and look at me as I am; thou hast seen such things that thou hast gained strength to bear my smile." I was like one that wakes from a forgotten dream and strives in vain to bring it again to mind when I heard this invitation, worthy of such gratitude that it can never be blotted from the book that records the past.[14]

The important point about Dante's dream psychology is that the emotional content remains even when the conceptual content of the dream-vision cannot be recalled. Thus like the joy of a dream, a mystical vision and prenatal contact with God all remain as desire, a desire impelling the soul to experience again its original pleasure. It fixes on one object or another, always unsatisfied but always in hope, unaware exactly of what it seeks but always able to judge the lesser good as inadequate because of the "imprinted passion" in its soul. This process is nothing else than the search for the divine beatitude, and with proper guidance of human experience and judgment on the one hand and law on the other, it reaches its goal:

From His hand, who regards it fondly before it is, comes forth, like a child that sports, tearful and smiling, the little simple soul that knows nothing, but, moved by a joyful maker, turns eagerly to what delights it. At first it tastes the savour of a trifling good; it is beguiled there and runs after it, if guide or curb do not divert its love. Therefore there was need for law to be set as a curb; there was need for a king who should discern at least the tower of the true city.[15]

In the characteristic manner in which the same themes appear and reappear as he sees more and more truth and achieves greater understanding as he approaches his goal, Dante refers in the *Paradiso* to the implanted love for the Creator which the soul acquires in that moment of contact with God when it was created:

The angels, brother, and the pure country where thou art may be said to be created just as they are in their entire being; but the elements thou hast named and those things that are made from them are given their form by created power. Created was the matter that is in them, created was the informing virtue in these stars that wheel about them. The soul of every beast and of the plants is drawn from a potential complex by the shining and motion of the holy lights; but your life the Supreme Beneficence breathes forth immediately, and He so enamours it of Himself that it desires Him ever after.[16]

Thus Dante, having experienced a true platonic love nostalgia, found an equivalent for the platonic notion of *anamnesis* in the doctrine of the special creation of each individual soul. The previous contact with the absolute came in the moment of its creation—not in a vision in a pre-existent state, itself one of an infinite series of such states interrupted by reincarnations.

Love in Dante thus appears not only in terms of the Augustinian doctrine of the weight of love (*pondus amoris*) fused with the Aristotelian doctrine of natural place, but in terms of nostalgia, the truly platonic note in love speculation. The kinds of love are not statically classified and distinguished but are in a dynamic and dialectical relationship to one another. Man is the focal point of every kind of love, including the love which he derives from his status as a part of nature and the love which impels him dialectically through and beyond the lower forms of love and springs from that moment of contact with God in the creation of his immortal and supernatural part. This love leads man to use creatures in order to ascend to a transcendent God through a natural process guided by judgment and law, forms of volitional discipline which order desire. The ascent through the scale of creatures arranged in a hierarchy of good and beautiful is nothing other than the dynamic nature of love itself, each grade in the ladder helping the pilgrim regain that half-remembered supreme beauty. Love carries intellect with it in this journey, expanding and enriching it, and intellect in turn feeds the flame of love.[17]

The main discourse of love is elaborated in the *Purgatorio* (XVI–XVIII) at the very center of the *Divine Comedy*. It is at the center because love itself is the "central" revealer of the universe, it is the heart of things in both the actual universe and the universe of the poem. In Canto XVIII Dante explains how implanted love operates on the natural level. Every soul is potentially capable of love, a love which can be actualized by perception of an object which is pleasing. This notion is already present in the tenth sonnet of the *Vita nuova*, "Amor e 'l cor gentil sono una cosa," in which Dante describes the love of a gentleman for a lady and how she actualizes the potentiality of love in her lover.

Dante in the following passage from *Purgatorio* XVIII fully explains how the process takes place. The intellect abstracts from the sensible forms conveyed to it through the senses the form or species (i.e., *intenzione*, l. 23) of a true or real being in the outside world (*esser verace*, l. 22). The intellect, after this process of abstraction takes place, presents this form to the will, which is free to incline itself to the object or not.

The mind, created quick to love, is readily moved towards everything that pleases, as soon as by the pleasure it is roused to action. Your perception takes from outward reality an impression and unfolds it within you, so that it makes the mind to turn to it; and if the mind, so turned, inclines to it, that inclination is love, that is nature, which by pleasure is bound on you afresh.[18]

This love is natural, not supernatural, as Virgil points out when he refers Dante to Beatrice for an explanation of that love to which reason cannot attain (ll. 46–48). The will is "bound again" in the sense that when it was in a potential state in regard to love it was "bound" the first time. After the potentiality of love has been actualized and the will has freely made its choice, it is "bound again" in that the will is fixed on the object of its desire. It wants the thing itself and cannot rest in pursuit of it. Dante emphasizes the naturalness of this process by comparing this kind of love to the natural movement of fire seeking its place.

Then, as fire moves upward by its form, being born to mount where it most abides in its matter, so the mind thus seized enters into desire, which is a spiritual movement, and never rests until the thing loved makes it rejoice.[19]

This impulse to love and the knowledge of primary ideas are in men as the impulse to make honey is in bees. There is no further explanation possible, in the sense that it cannot be deduced from man's rational essence. This primary natural love is innocent in its impulse, and a man is not guilty in terms of a natural impulse. We possess, however, a faculty of judgment which counsels the impulse of natural desire by assenting or denying. "This is the principle in which is found the reason of desert in you according as it garners and winnows out good and guilty loves." Natural impulses of desire arise from necessity, but the will is free and it is in man's power to control it.

Therefore, whence come the knowledge of primary ideas and the bent to the primary objects of desire, no man knows; they are in you just as in bees zeal to make honey, and this primal will admits no deserving of praise or blame. Now in order that to this will every other may be conformed there is innate in you the faculty which counsels and which ought to hold the threshold of assent. This is the principle in which is found the reason of desert in you according as it garners and winnows out good and guilty loves. Those who in their reasoning went to the root recognized this innate freedom and therefore left ethics to the world. Admitting then that every love that is kindled in you arises of necessity, the power to control it is in you; that noble faculty Beatrice means by freewill and therefore see thou have it in mind if she would speak of it to thee.[20]

The description of the process found here is substantially the same as that common in the schools and described by Aquinas. Love is something which pertains to the appetite and can be classified according to the kinds of appetites. There is the kind of appetition which does not follow its own apprehension, namely, the simple natural impulse. This is the natural appetite of creatures without knowledge, directed to their ends by a higher knower or "by the apprehension of another." There is the kind of appetition which follows immediately upon apprehension, and this is sensitive appetite. It is of necessity, and not of free will, the possession of dumb animals. In man, however, this same sensitive appetite appears in a different form, where it participates in a kind of freedom to the extent that it may obey reason. The third and highest kind of appetition is that following upon the apprehension of a creature possessing free choice (*secundum liberum arbitrium*), and this is rational, intellective appetition or will (*voluntas*). In each and every case, love may be called the principle of motion tending toward the goal that is loved (*principium motus tendentis in finem amatum*). St. Thomas goes on to explain that the principle of this motion in natural love or appetition is a certain "connaturality." In the higher forms, the appetition of the sensitive nature or of the faculty of will, the principle of motion is a certain "co-aptation" or "complacency" of and in the good. We might perhaps express this "complacency" as a singular and particular affinity for a particular good, as distinct from generalized desire for goodness.[21]

St. Thomas gives a further explanation of what he means by these terms in a discussion of whether or not love is a "passion." A passion is the affect of an agent in the patient or that upon which it acts. This agent confers both form and the motion consequent upon that form, so that, for example, in the process of generation the agent gives to a body its weight and the motion following upon that weight. This principle of weight (*gravitas*) is the principle of motion of a body to a place which is "connatural" to it because of the kind of weight it has. Thomas says, with his usual suspicion of anything that suggests the metaphorical use of language, that this may be called natural "love" in a manner of speaking (*quoddammodo dici amor naturalis*), just as he was willing to grant to the metaphysicians of light their use of metaphors of light to describe spiritual and intellectual matters so long as they were aware they were using figurative language. Analogously, the object of appetition gives to the faculty of appetition, first, a kind of "coaptation" which is complacency in the object of appetite (*complacentia appetibilis*) and, second, motion toward it.

Thus appetition acts in a pattern which may be described as circular. The object of appetite acts as the efficient cause when the faculty receives the form which assimilates it to the object and as the final cause when the object elicits motion toward itself. This reception of the form, species, or "intention" of the object of appetite in the faculty of appetition is the first change brought about by the object of desire in the subject. It is the result of "complacency" in the object of appetition. The motion following upon this is desire, and the ultimate rest which follows upon attainment of the object is joy.[22] This whole analysis, it becomes clear, is an attempt to explain why we like some things, how we come to feel an affinity for what we actually in each instance want.

St. Thomas' language here is quite technical, and I have expounded him in his own terms before explaining the relevance of these texts to the passage from the *Purgatorio* (XVIII, 19 ff.) because his meaning will become clearer if we see the way in which Dante rendered these concepts. The term *piacere* in line 27 (cf. Provençal *plazer*, "attraction," "charm"), often translated as "pleasing impression," is actually a translation of the Latin *complacentia*. In the lower kinds of substances there is the implanted natural affinity for them to seek their proper place. This affinity, which follows upon the apprehension of a higher knower who directs them to their ends, St. Thomas calls connaturality. The higher analogue in the realm of appetition is *complacentia*, not active desire but what might be called *awareness of desirability*, a certain coaptation of the appetite for its object, the necessary presupposition of motion toward it or of desire for it. *Complacentia* is the first change which the object of appetition induces in the subject and consists of the reception in the subject of the "intention" (l. 23) or form. This reception creates an affinity in the subject for the object, it "coapts" him to the object. The same thing which is the cause of creating this affinity is also its final cause, inducing active desire. Thus the circularity of the process of love, the closing of the circle being accompanied by rest and joy. The pattern of love in Dante is also circular, or perhaps spiral, each step in the ladder to God closing one circular movement and initiating another —increase of good and beauty increasing love which in turn demands a higher good.

The analogous process takes place on every level of reality. Active desire is the higher analogue, on the conscious level of motion, to natural place on the lower level. Conscious affinity, accompanied by pleasure, is the higher analogue of the natural unconscious affinity of insentient creatures for their natural place. In the insentient order natural appetition is unconscious and unwilled; in the order of sensation without rationality it is conscious and unwilled; in man it is willed and conscious.[23]

But desire in man has a further peculiarity precisely because it is the desire of a rational being. Man, by nature, desires the eternal, or immortality, in which alone the higher faculties can find the rest and joy that are the goal of all desire. A sign of immortality is that the natural desire for it cannot be in vain. The will of any rational creature naturally desires the eternal because reason, unlike sense, is not confined to the "here and now" but knows without being confined to either time or place. It knows "absolutely" and, in a sense, "timelessly." Its mode of existence being thus spaceless and timeless it naturally desires eternal existence.[24]

Dante makes significant use of this doctrine of desire for the eternal. Speaking of the beauty of the angelic lady, he says that he intends to speak of her in the aspect in which the goodness of her soul reveals itself as sensible beauty. This beauty is such that things are revealed through it which demonstrate some of the joys of Paradise. The noblest of joys is to be content, which is nothing less than to be blessed. This kind of blessedness or contentment is found in the sensible beauty of the lady who is perfect in her species, but it is different from what would be felt in Paradise because it is interrupted and not everlasting.[25]

So in *Paradiso* XXIV Beatrice invokes the blessed as those eternally satisfied:

O fellowship elect to the great supper of the blessed Lamb, who feeds you so that your desire is ever satisfied, since by God's grace this man has foretaste of that which falls from your table, before death appoints his time, give heed to his measureless craving and bedew him with some drops; you drink always from the fountain whence comes that on which his mind is set.[26]

As the beauty of the lady in the *Convivio* fed the eyes of her beholders, giving them a foretaste of the joys of Paradise, so Beatrice in Paradise asks for more food from the supper of the lamb for Dante, who is having a foretaste of the joys which his measureless craving desires.

This measureless craving, this desire for eternal possession of good or beauty, is a function of the rational soul, of man's natural desire for possession of eternal good in an eternal existence. So much is common to both Dante and the schools. The important difference between them on this matter is that for Dante sensible human beauty is the highest temporal analogue of the perpetual joys and contentment of the eternal existence man desires. This satisfaction which is the goal of man's desire is a union of peace and ardor, tranquility and passion, a passionate tranquility in which desire finds rest without in some sense ceasing to be desire—a state which in Paradise cannot be lost and which requires no effort to retain.

The correlate of love is beauty, and we must now examine in greater detail what beauty in its various forms, corporeal and incorporeal, is for Dante, showing how it operates and what is its purpose.

All medieval speculation on the nature of love and beauty was ultimately platonic and neoplatonic, and the transmission of this classical stock of ideas was in great part the work of the church fathers. For the Middle Ages perhaps the most important sources for these doctrines are the writings of St.

Augustine and the works of Pseudo-Dionysius, especially the fourth chapter of the latter's *De divinis nominibus*.[27] That the complex of ideas which constituted Greek speculation on these matters was not passively received has been generally clear, but some of the important modifications they under-went in their transmission seem to have been overlooked. One of them is the Augustinian reinterpretation of Plotinian ideas on the nature of beauty. St. Augustine's ideas on aesthetics had a profound influence on medieval thinkers and, as will be seen, provided the Middle Ages with the basic concepts necessary for a revaluation of the role and nature of human beauty, a revaluation which reached its greatest expression in the work of Dante. Let us first turn briefly to Plotinus and then see what changes St. Augustine made in his theory of beauty.

For Plotinus beauty was one of the aspects under which being could be considered. Any corporeal substance was beautiful by virtue of the ideal essence—that form which is both the principle of being and intelligibility—shining in and through its sensuous phenomena. A body is the copy of the Idea which has manifested itself in matter. The entire world of the senses is beautiful because it is through this embodiment of the archetypal forms that the spiritual light streams into the world of matter.[28] Before Plotinus, the beautiful had gen-erally appeared only in unison with the good and perfect or, as in Aristotle, had been conceived in relation to ethical ef-fects. Plotinus thus made what is apparently the first success-ful attempt at a metaphysics of beauty.

St. Augustine accepted this metaphysical estimate of the nature of beauty, but did not relegate beauty to a status, along with being, below the "One." Rather, the archetypes are in God, and in his unity are found, elevated to the state of per-fect simplicity and infinity, all the perfections of which we receive a glimpse in this world. For both Plotinus and St. Augustine, however, beauty is a function of that principle which constitutes things in their being and their intelligibility. In this they agree. But St. Augustine gave to beauty a purpose in the order of things absent in Plotinus. Its primary function is to make known the Creator, and it is the way the divine *primarily* manifests itself in irrational creatures, whereas in rational creatures the divine is primarily present as the power to know, as reason itself. The irrational creatures, animals and plants especially, are not able to know (*noscere* or *nosse*), but they seem to want to make known (*innotescere*) their Creator, the verb *innotescere* being virtually synonymous with *notum facere*.

This is the central point of a striking passage from the *City of God* on how God is found in creatures. St. Augustine begins by explaining that human nature so loves knowing and so dislikes being deceived that every man should rather lament with a sane mind than rejoice in madness. This rational power belongs to man alone and does not exist in the other animals. Although some of the irrational animals may have a keener sight for the kind of light found in this world, material light, they cannot attain to that incorporeal light with which our minds are somehow irradiated, the kind of spiritual light which enables us to form judgments concerning all things. Indeed, our power to judge is directly proportional to the extent that we possess this light.

Although irrational animals do not have knowledge, they seem to have something which bears a resemblance to knowledge (*quaedam scientiae similitudo*) in their faculties of sensation. Other corporeal creatures are called sensible not because they possess the faculty of sensation but because they are objects of sensation. Yet even among plants, their ability to nourish themselves, to grow and reproduce, has some resemblance to sensation. The causes of these and of all other corporeal things lie hidden in their natures. Their forms (*formas*), however, in virtue of which the structure of this visible world is beautiful (*formosa*), they proffer to our senses, as if to compensate for their lack of knowledge by making known their Creator. We see the image of God by looking within and knowing that we are, delighting in our being and our knowledge of it. The irrational orders cannot do this, but they can manifest the image of God through their beauty.

I would like to call particular attention to the manner in which the word *forma* meaning the *species* of a thing, its principle of being and intelligibility, provides the adjective *formosa*, beautiful. Thus the corporeal things of this world whose forms we perceive make the visible universe beautiful. Such sensible forms are perceived by our bodily senses, but we do not judge of them by such senses. For we possess a sense, far superior to the bodily senses, a sense which belongs to the inner man, by means of which we perceive what things are just and unjust—just by means of an intelligible form (*species*), unjust by the privation or lack of such a form.[29]

The meaning of the term *innotescere* becomes clearer when St. Augustine uses it in a refutation of the Academic skeptical argument concerning the deceptive nature of sensation. He says that we must not doubt that what we learn through the corporeal senses is true, for through them we learn about both heaven and earth. Indeed, all things that we know in the heavens and on the earth are known by us to the extent that He who created both them and us wishes to make them known to us (*innotescere nobis voluit*). Here the term is used not with an aesthetic but with a purely epistemological significance. Both beauty and knowledge, therefore, are forms of "making known" the Creator, and the principle which makes an object knowable is the same one that makes it beautiful.[30]

As the word *forma*, the principle of being and cognition in a thing, has the adjective *formosa*, beautiful, so its synonym *species* has the adjective *speciosa* also meaning beautiful. We are here not dealing with a merely verbal similarity. Language itself is simply a testimony of this derivation of beauty from the form or species of a thing. Even the lowest *species* is from God, and it is not, therefore, adventitious that the Supreme Being is praised by the adjective *formosissimus et speciosissimus*, meaning most beautiful but also most real, having the utmost possible form.[31]

Created beings reflect as much of the divine perfections as is proper to their degree. The soul which loves God above all is free to possess a corporeal thing so that it may be a kind of final good. The thing is beautiful after its kind (*in genere suo pulchrum*) in virtue of the fact that it carries the impress of, or is constituted by, the form or species,[32] and it is beautiful precisely because its inner essence, its immaterial *species*, has fully stamped itself on matter. It is for this reason that a beautiful thing is called *speciosa* or *formosa*.[33] Whatever we may think of St. Augustine's semantics, it is clear that he is identifying the principle of beauty with the principle of being and intelligibility.

This beauty which shines forth in creation is ultimately to be understood as a reflex of the divine beauty. When we regard the Creator by whom all things are made and who is understood by the things that are made (Rom. 1: 20), we must understand the Trinity of whom there appear traces in the creature and who is the supreme source of all things, the most perfect beauty and the most blessed delight.[34] The interrelationship between the persons of the Trinity also reveals something of the nature of beauty. St. Augustine explains that when Hilary called the Son the image (*imago*) and *species* of the Father he meant that the Son is called the *species* because he is a perfect image, in perfect correspondence to the Father, and that such an image is beautiful. For when an image corresponds perfectly to that of which it is an image, it perfectly realizes its form, thereby engendering beauty.[35] Thus a similar situation obtains between the persons of the Trinity as obtains between the archetypes of things in the mind of God and the things themselves.[36]

In a magnificent passage in a commentary on Psalm 144, St. Augustine again discusses the revealing power of beauty, its power to reveal its source, and again equates *species* as the principle of being with *pulchrum*, the most common term for beauty. God ordered his creation like the steps of a ladder extending from earth to heaven, from the visible to the invisible, from the mortal to the immortal. This interwoven connection of creatures, this most ordered beauty (*pulchritudo*) rising from the bottom of the scale to the top and descending from the top to the very bottom without any interruptions in continuity, but tempered with difference and variety (*sed dissimilibus temperata*), all of this—this totality—praises God. Why does it do so? Because when you regard it and find it to be beautiful (*pulchrum vides*) you are praising God in it, you are admiring him in his creation. The beauty of the earth (*species terrae*) is a kind of silent voice, the voice of the dumb earth proclaiming its Creator. Look at it and see its beauty (*speciem*), its fecundity, its creative power, how it receives seed and how it also brings forth even more without being sown. We must look at the earth and reflect upon it as if we were questioning it, and this examination of it is itself a questioning.[37]

The beauty of creation arranged in a hierarchy of greater

and greater beauty leading to God thus possesses revealing power, especially the power of revealing God. To say this is to say that beauty yields knowledge, but knowledge of a special sort, knowledge of the *Deus Artifex* who created that beauty, indeed who is that beauty. Beauty not only reveals God but also functions as a lure, as a kind of attractive power forcing the spirit up toward God. So in the *Confessions*, St. Augustine tells us that he was rapt and drawn up to God by his beauty, but soon was torn away by his own spiritual weight, unable to stay and enjoy God when he finally found him (*et non stabam frui Deo meo, sed rapiebar ad te decore tuo, moxque diripiebar abs te pondere meo*). His weight or love was not of the right kind to establish for long his "natural place" with God. God's beauty seized him for an instant, but his weight pulled him down again because it was of this world.[38]

St. Augustine thus had been to the true homeland of the soul, God himself, by whom it was created and from whom it comes forth, brought to that exalted "place" by God's beauty.[39] All lesser beauties—even a man's very vices—serve but to *remind* us of that primal beauty the soul abandoned and to lead us back to him.[40] In his wisdom, God, the supreme artificer, interwove and co-ordinated all of his works, to the end that they be beautiful. So the supreme goodness has no envy of any lesser beauty since all beauty is from him, from the lowest to the highest.[41]

The ladder of beauty also has a subjective aspect, for if we consider the manner in which we judge external corporeal beauty we are necessarily driven to the conception of an immaterial standard by which we judge it. This internal standard we possess is, however, mutable, so that we are again driven to posit a beauty which is eternal and immutable. There is no corporeal beauty (*pulchritudo*) at all, whether it be a function of the shape and configuration of body or of its movement, as in music, which mind alone does not judge. The mind, however, would not be able to do this if it did not possess a superior form of this beauty (*nisi melior in illo esset haec species*), a beauty without mass, without the clamor of speech, without space, place, or time.

St. Augustine then proceeds to demonstrate how the personal inner "beauty" which serves as our basis of judgment must be mutable and how we are forced to infer the existence of an immutable standard. Men vary by nature and training in their capacity to exercise judgment regarding sensible beauty (*de specie sensibili*), and the same man judges better after he has gained experience than before. Therefore gifted and learned men who have deeply studied these matters have concluded that the primal beauty (*primam speciem*) is not in those things which are mutable. When these men saw that body and mind could be more or less beautiful (*speciosa*) and that if they were lacking in beauty (*omni specie carere*) they would have no existence whatsoever (*omnino nulla essent*), they rightly inferred the existence of a first principle which is immutable and admits of no degrees of comparison. They rightly believed that this first principle was uncreated and the creator of all things. Paraphrasing St. Paul (Rom. 1: 19–20), St. Augustine concludes the argument by saying that what is known of God he manifested to men when they saw his invisible things through understanding his visible ones, rising to his eternal power and divinity through all visible and temporal things he created.

In the Latin text the term *species* and its derivatives carry both an ontological and aesthetic meaning. Indeed, St. Augustine's argument is fundamentally the proof for the existence of God from contingency. From the mutable nature of all things we must infer an immutable, eternal being on which

their being depends. St. Augustine, however, is also arguing
from the nature of beauty at the same time, merging both
proofs by means of the particular meanings he makes his terms
carry. This, as we have seen, was made possible by his conception of the relation between beauty and the formal principle which constitutes the being and intelligibility of things.[42]
Thus, by contemplating corporeal beauty, the mind is forced
to turn in upon itself to find an even higher beauty. It cannot
rest at this stage, however, and must go even further until it
arrives at that uncreated beauty who created all the lower
forms through which the mind had passed on its upward
journey.

These Augustinian ideas we have considered exerted a great
influence during the medieval period, especially on the thinkers of the school of St. Victor, on Alexander of Hales, and,
via him, on St. Bonaventura. Alexander used as the point
of departure for his speculations on the nature of beauty one
of the Augustinian triads: *modus, species,* and *ordo.*[43] This
triad first appears in the Augustinian corpus in his treatise
De natura boni, where he classifies the kinds of good found
in all created things, kinds which all proceed from God who
is the author of all good. "Mode," "beauty," and "order" are
three such goods, beauty being therefore a subdivision of the
good, almost but not quite a synonym of good, rendered by
the term *species.*[44]

Alexander especially emphasized the second term of this
triad and started a new direction in medieval thought on the
nature of beauty. Beauty proceeds from form in its external
relationship as the principle which makes a thing please by
its aspect. Alexander prescinds it from any of the utilitarian
relationships that a form may have with other things or with
ourselves. Insofar as the form is what it should be, insofar
as it conforms to the wisdom of God who created it, it is

ontologically true. When it so conforms, the form is in its fullness. This fullness of form radiates from the object in its sensible aspect and makes that object beautiful.[45]

This aesthetic principle was also merged with various ideas in the light-metaphysics tradition. Indeed, the language used to describe the fullness of form which is beauty was the language of light, like *splendor, fulgor,* and *claritas.* One reason for this fusion of ideas lay in the fact that for the "metaphysicians of light," light was both the principle of form and the principle of beauty. Grosseteste, for example, refers to light as the *species* and perfection of all bodies, the term *species* carrying the meaning of beauty as well as form: *Species et perfectio corporum omnium est lux.*[46] Again, in *De unica forma omnium* he equates *pulchrum, speciosum,* and *formosum,* deriving beauty from the radiance of that light which constitutes the form of the object, and concludes with the observation that God as the form over all forms is the most perfect, beautiful, and complete of beings.[47]

St. Bonaventura both employed and elaborated the Augustinian aesthetic and the concept of a ladder of beauty. Indeed, the universe itself is nothing but a ladder to God.[48] God is, of course, at the very pinnacle of this ladder, the supreme unity and good without beginning. He is also the supreme truth and, because he is the supreme truth, also supremely simple, uniform (*aequale*), and beautiful. Moreover, his beauty is a function of his truth and "equality." [49]

There is for St. Bonaventura another, more metaphorical way of considering the ladder of beauty by which it is seen to lead from the beauty of the world, through the beauty of the Church adorned with the grace of its saints, to the beauty of heaven, and finally to the "supermaximal" beauty of the Trinity.[50] Indeed, it is the function of beauty—along with other qualities of the created world—to proclaim God's power, wisdom, and goodness (*immensitas potentiae sapientiae et bonitatis trini Dei*). The earthly beauty which proclaims these attributes of the Divinity is a function of the light, configurations and colors of simple, mixed, and even composite bodies, i.e., the celestial bodies, minerals, stones, metals, plants, and animals.[51]

All things knowable generate their intelligible species, and in this they are, as it were, mirrors of the eternal generation of the Son from the Father. The intelligible species gives us joy as the beautiful (*speciosa*), and from this we can infer that the primal beauty is "primal species" (*in illa prima specie est prima speciositas*). Joy is the conjunction of a thing with something which fits that thing, and, since the likeness of God to himself is the highest beauty (*summe speciosi*), we can infer from this that he possesses true joy and that all other lesser joys lead us back to him. St. Bonaventura thus argues that beauty is discerned when the intelligible species is apprehended. This apprehension is accompanied by joy because it is a harmonious union of the intelligible species with the mind, of a reality with something that fits that reality.

Like St. Augustine, St. Bonaventura shifts between the epistemological and ontological leanings of *species* and its derivatives and the aesthetic meaning. The assimilation of knower to known which is the very process of knowledge is accompanied by joy because it is a harmonious union of the intelligible form which constitutes the being of the object with the intellect of the knowing subject. This process is at the same time the apprehension of beauty as well as knowledge. Now similitude, as we have seen in St. Augustine, is the principle of beauty. To the extent that a thing resembles its archetype, its idea, to that extent it is beautiful. But the Word is Similitude itself, and therefore Beauty itself. Since, however, the Son is in perfect correspondence to the Father in a harmonious union, deficient in no way, perfect joy must be present in the Trinity. Thus by a consideration of the process of apprehension St. Bonaventura argues that the function of beauty and of the joy which arises from its perception is to lead us to the true joy and beauty of God.[52] Perhaps St. Bonaventura's most beautiful description of the meaning and function of beauty is contained in his laudation of St. Francis who

beheld in fair things Him who is most fair, and through the traces of Himself that He hath imprinted on His creatures, he everywhere followed on to search the Beloved, making of all things a ladder for himself whereby he might ascend to lay hold on Him who is altogether lovely. For by impulse of his unexampled devotion he tasted that fountain of goodness that streamed forth, as in rivulets, in every created thing, and perceived as it were an heavenly harmony in the concord of the virtues and actions granted unto them by God, and did sweetly exhort them to praise the Lord, even as the Prophet David had done.[53]

The various speculations on the nature and function of beauty we have been considering were related to light speculation from the very beginning, when Plotinus maintained that it was through the embodiment of the archetypal forms in matter that spiritual light radiated into the material world. In thirteenth-century thought, the relationship between beauty and light was very close and was especially developed in the tradition of light metaphysics. In this period, metaphysical and physical doctrines concerning light as the principle of beauty, or of that "fullness" of form or being which is beauty, were paralleled in the realms of medieval art and literature by an extraordinary attention to light and color. It has often been remarked that the Gothic cathedral is "weightless." Its lines run up and finally curve into space, and its interior is designed to make the most effective possible use of light and color. Medieval painting and illumination witness to the extraordinary attention artists gave to color, and one of the outstanding characteristics of romance poetry in the Middle Ages is the aptness of the old French and Provençal poets in seizing on luminous details. In their lyrics great attention is given to the color of flowers and trees, the contrast of light and shade, the color of the beloved's hair and eyes. Even if, as in most cases, these descriptions are conventional, the poetic remains one of visual quality.[54] The *Chanson de Roland*, a long poem, is also filled with details of light and color. Durendal and Precieuse gleam in the sunlight; the ensigns and standards of the warriors shine brightly in their various colors; the chamber of King Marsilies is elaborately and brilliantly painted. There is scarcely a bodily characteristic which is not rendered in terms of light and color: the whiteness of skin, redness of blood, whiteness of beards, and blondness of hair.

Edgar De Bruyne calls attention to the frequency with which feminine beauty is celebrated among the trouvères and troubadours in terms of light and color. As he observes, this interest in the luminous and colorful on the part of these poets is not necessarily intrinsically related to the metaphysics and physics of light, but the latter does afford a kind of conceptual justification of what we might call a poetic of luminous and colorful detail. Light is the source of all beauty because, in the view of the "light metaphysicians," it constitutes the very being of things, and what we admire in a beautiful body is really that light which constitutes its extension and shape.[55]

Emile Legouis made this conception of a poetic of light the basis of his defense of French poetry. He justly remarks that the instinctive preference of the romance poets for detail of light and color is in striking contrast to the atmosphere of *Beowulf* and that this preference has remained a characteristic of the main tradition of French poetry. The *Chanson de Roland* is the only song of disaster in the genre to be painted entirely in gay colors.[56]

Both in the intuitive poetic of light and in the conceptual metaphysics of light, all beauty was conceived as primarily visual and luminous, and this included human as well as natural beauty. But all beauty is a reflection of divine beauty, and, therefore, that beauty which is found in a person is a true good and a mirror of divine beauty. Guibert of Nogent in *De vita sua*, speaking of the beauty of women says: *Omne illud quod temporaliter speciosum est, aeternae speciei quasi speculum est.*[57] Thus the beauty of a woman may be a revelation of divine beauty, although it may be badly understood, loved, and admired and thereby become a means of destruction. Beauty and love are a function of each other, and therefore human love, properly directed and understood, will be transformed into the love of God. For beauty is distributed throughout a hierarchy of luminous incarnations (*specula*) —the created universe—of which one reflects the other because all reflect God. Love also presents itself in a multitude of analogical forms. To Guibert and later others such as Nicholas of Cusa, the woman is one of these incarnations, and human love may thus be the initiation of a love for the divine.[58]

Guibert sees in bodily beauty both a reflection of divine beauty and the beauty of the soul. It may be recalled that the soul of a person is his substantial form or species, so that human as well as natural beauty is also that "fullness" of form which translates itself through sensible particulars.[59] St. Bernard shared this view of the nature of human beauty, but for him the emphasis is on spiritual beauty of soul, a beauty it possesses through being an image of the divine infinity.

It is this spiritual beauty which is represented in allegorical form in the Song of Solomon. Man turns within and in contemplating the beauty of his soul mounts, by a kind of reflex act, to the beauty of his Creator.[60]

To St. Bernard the perception of sensible beauty fills the soul with longing for that beauty which is immutable; it engenders a melancholy dissatisfaction with the beauty of corruptible things and initiates a quest for eternal beauty. It engenders a love nostalgia.[61] True human beauty is spiritual and internal, for it is the soul which possesses the image of God. Indeed, whatever external beauty there is in the human being—the beauty of his body—is simply a radiation from the luminous beauty of the soul. If the soul of a person has not obliterated or defaced the divine image within it and has interior grace, it will manifest its spiritual beauty as an exterior grace of action and expression.[62]

Important passages in the *Convivio* of Dante become clear when read in the light of these ultimately Plotinian-Augustinian ideas on the nature and function of beauty. In Book III, viii, Dante says that he is going to speak of his angelic lady and tell us of how the goodness of her soul is revealed to the observer as sensible beauty. Beauty is an external light that makes manifest an internal splendor, an internal light. Dante then uses this principle to explain the beauty of a creature who is the highest perfection of her species. In such a person the soul is of such a high degree of goodness that its beauty is made to appear visibly in her body. Let us recall again that the soul of man is his *species*, the form which constitutes his being, and that this *species* is continually radiating or generating the *species* which is the object of the human faculty of apprehension. As St. Bonaventura said along with so many others, this *species* gives us pleasure as beauty and creates joy in him who apprehends it, a joy which resembles the joy existing in the Triune Creator. In a creature like the lady who is perfect in her *species*, the joy engendered is of such a high degree that it is a foretaste of the joys of paradise; the only difference between the joy of beholding such a creature and the joys of paradise are that the latter are perpetual.[63]

Dante's doctrine of the internal and external lights of beauty is made clearer in his discussion of the beauty of the smile of this angelic lady. Her soul reveals itself through the mouth as color through glass, and what is the smile or laughter but a coruscation of the soul's joy, an external light which is an image of the internal light? [64] Indeed, man is called a divine animal by the philosophers precisely because the rational soul is so spiritual, so free from, or superior to, the sheer potentiality which is matter that the divine light, the ultimate source of the splendor of the soul, can shine through it.[65] Dante thus mingles the Augustinian notion of beauty as the translation through sensible particulars of the informing principle with the conception of light as the principle of beauty. The same *species* which is the principle of knowledge, being, and beauty is itself a kind of light, for the metaphysicians of light conceived of *lux* as the principle of being, knowledge, and beauty. It therefore follows that the most beautiful parts of the body are those in which the soul, the divine light, is most active—the eyes and the mouth, balconies looking in upon the dwelling places of the soul.[66]

The special beauty of the eyes and mouth is ordained by the special love the soul bears toward those parts. In turn, this love is a part of the operation of that universal principle of love, of love as a cosmic principle, which inclines all things to love and be loved and which ordains the soul to beautify especially the eyes and mouth.[67] Thus the love which is the key to the universe orders both love and the objects of love, ordaining what things shall be beautiful and in what degree. The beauty of the smiling lips appeals to the eyes, not that they may be fed as if vision were like the sense of taste, but rather that it may elicit love, a love which is a special case of universal love, helping to initiate a process which begins in a vision of beauty and ends in a vision of paradise.

The circle is thus closed: the ladders of love and beauty are conceptually unified in the all-inclusive idea of universal love ordering to each other the forms of love and the manifestations of beauty. This all-embracing principle of love is the same Love in whose presence Dante assumes the circular movement of eternity, the Love which moves the sun and other stars. The soul, the noblest of all the manifestations of divine perfection, travels restlessly through all the relatively good and beautiful things of this world seeking a beauty which is not of this world. Spurred on by a love nostalgia and guided in its quest by judgment, the soul will attain that perfect joy and satisfaction which is blessedness. The beauty of the beloved person, the angelic lady, is so perfect that it is virtually equal to the immaterial and higher beauty of the angels. Such a beauty is the meeting point between corporeal beauty and spiritual beauty in the hierarchy of incarnations of beauty leading to God. Such beauty arouses both joy and bewilderment, joy in "reminding" the lover of beauty, bewilderment because his "remembering" is still mixed with "forgetfulness," with ignorance of its true source. The lover thus begins his ascent toward true and eternal beauty, unsure of his goal but committed to the flight. As he ascends, the meaning of his flight becomes clearer and clearer. The love which seemed an irrational impulse and the beauty which seemed a holy mystery are both understood in the intuition of universal love and of absolute beauty.

IV

Dante and the Pauline Modes of Vision

ST. PAUL, the "chosen vessel of the Holy Spirit" as Dante calls him in the twenty-first canto of the *Paradiso*, expanding the famous epithet in the Acts of the Apostles, had the most controversial if not the earliest Christian mystical experience. This is the experience he describes in the Second Epistle to the Corinthians, and it was to be the point of departure and reference for much of later mystical and theological speculation. St. Paul describes his rapture as follows:

I knew a man in Christ above fourteen years ago (whether in the body, I cannot tell; or whether out of the body, I cannot tell:

God knoweth;), such an one caught up to the third heaven. And I knew such a man (whether in the body, or out of the body, I cannot tell: God knoweth;) how that he was caught up into paradise, and heard unspeakable words which it is not lawful for a man to utter.[1]

The question arose as to the precise nature of St. Paul's rapture. Did St. Paul actually see God in his essence and nature? Or was he granted a vision of many divine things short of a direct and immediate vision of God? Indeed, can any man in this life attain to that beatific vision, even for an instant, which is the prerogative of the angels and saints? In the fourth century, St. Gregory Nazianzen decided that no man in this life could know what God is in his essence and nature. This would be possible only after our mortal minds have been divinized, after the image or copy which is the mind has ascended to its divine exemplar. Indeed, the very question widely discussed among the theologians turns on the proposition that we are sometime going to know as we are known. In this mortal life all we grasp of God is as a narrow rivulet or a small ray of that great light. Therefore all claims, including scriptural ones, of having seen God are to be interpreted in some relative way, as a participation in which others share less.[2]

St. Gregory Nazianzen alludes to another famous Pauline text concerning knowledge of God in this world and the next: "For now we see as through a glass, darkly; but then face to face: now I know in part; but then shall I know even also as I am known." [3] He uses St. Paul himself as an authority against the possibility of seeing the divine essence while still in this life.

The Pauline text just cited was eventually interpreted with the aid of another one from Romans: "For the invisible things of him from the creation of the world are clearly seen, being understood by the things that are made, even his eternal power and Godhead." [4] These two texts were related by equating *speculum* with *creatura mundi*. The created world was a mirror of God, and everything in it reflected in some degree, by analogy, some aspect of the Creator. This is the knowledge whereby we glimpse the cause in its effects, for the similitude of the cause shines through the effects.[5] *Speculatio*, seeing God through his creatures, is a natural process in which all men share, and it simply requires a clear head, not sanctity or any special grace.

In the sixth century, the enormous weight of the authority of St. Gregory the Great was placed in support of the view that no man can see God in his essence in this life. Even if there are certain individuals living in the corruptible flesh who attained an incalculable power through the piercingness of their contemplation so that they were able to see the eternal brightness of God, this is not to be understood as being at variance with the words of Job that "Wisdom is hidden from the eyes of all the living." He who sees Wisdom dies to life and is not held by the love of life. The very circumstance of seeing God is death, for whether by the intention of the heart or by active carrying out, he who sees is separated with all his mind from the gratifications of this life. Hence it was said to Moses, "No man shall see me and live," which is to say that no man ever sees God spiritually and lives to the world carnally. So St. Paul, who saw the invisible things of God, in part, died to the world.[6] This argument is ambiguous and permits of a twofold interpretation. It would seem as if Gregory were allowing that some might see God in some special way, but he seems to exclude Moses and St. Paul from any essential vision of God. The problem rests on what St. Gregory means by seeing the eternal brightness of God.[7]

Whatever St. Gregory may have meant in this passage, the main direction of his thought is clear. The mist of human corruption obscures the incorruptible light and makes it inaccessible to our vision. The very fact that this light can in part be seen and simultaneously not be seen is simply a measure of how distant it is from us.[8] Similarly, commenting on Ezekiel 2: 1 (A.V., 1: 28), the phrase "the appearance of the likeness of the glory of the Lord," St. Gregory is careful to point out that Ezekiel does not say the vision of the glory but likeness of the glory. Ezekiel's intention in making this distinction was to show that no effort of the human mind, even if it represses bodily images in its thoughts and removes from the eyes of its heart all finite spirits, can attain to a vision of the glory of God as it is and still remain in mortal flesh. That which shines in the mind is no more than a likeness. Thus St. Paul, who was rapt to the third heaven itself, said that we now see through a glass darkly.[9]

It is interesting to observe that, for St. Gregory, the rapture of Paul is virtually equated with the indirect vision of God *per speculum*. For him, even the ascent to the third heaven did not imply anything more than an indirect vision of God. St. Paul saw much more than ordinary men see, perhaps, but his vision was still indirect.

St. Augustine, to whom we now turn and who claimed that both Moses and Paul had seen God in his essence, does not identify the vision of Paul's rapture with the indirect vision of God "as through a glass darkly." Rather it was a vision "face to face." In this rapture St. Paul canceled, by his own experience, the sharp distinction he drew between our knowledge of God in this life and in the next.

As St. Gregory the Great was the most important authority in the patristic period of those who claimed that no man in this life could see God in his essence, St. Augustine was the most important of those who claimed the opposite. But before we examine his views, let us consider still another text from St. Paul of which St. Augustine makes significant use. This is also from the Second Epistle to the Corinthians and makes an important distinction between faith and vision. St. Paul says: "Therefore we are always confident, knowing that, whilst we are at home in the body, we are absent from the Lord: (For we walk by faith, not by sight:)." [10] The distinction in this text, as St. Augustine interpreted it, is between knowing God through faith and knowing God in his essence. Indeed, this interpretation is quite plausible, since *species* translates the Greek *eidos* which can have the meaning essence in a philosophical context. The difference between *per fidem* and *per speciem* is parallel and analogous to the difference between *per speculum* and *facie ad faciem*. Of course, knowledge *per fidem* is a far more complete knowledge than that *per speculum*, since the created universe does not disclose upon examination the saving truths of Christian revelation. However, to know God *per speciem* would seem, for St. Augustine, to be the same as knowing him *facie ad faciem*, that is, in his essence.

Let us now turn to the texts in which St. Augustine argues his case that God can be seen in his essence. His first example is Moses, who with St. Paul is a classic example for the discussion of this problem. Earlier, St. Gregory of Nyssa maintained that Moses had had a vision of God in his essence, and St. Augustine is probably drawing on a long tradition of speculation on this matter. [11] Moses wanted greatly to see God, not as he was seen on the mountain or as he was seen in the temple, but in that substance by which he is God, not through any corporeal and creatural shape available to the senses or through any similitudes drawn from corporeal things even though seen with the spirit, but by his "species," in his essence—insofar as a rational and intellectual creature can grasp it—free of all bodily sense and all meaningful image (*aenigma*) of the spirit. In that "species" through which he is God, he speaks "ineffably secretly," and immediately in an ineffable language, speaks in that place where whoever sees him will not live with the mortal life of the bodily senses. Unless a man is in some sense dead to this life, whether wholly departed from the body as in death or so withdrawn from it that he does not know whether he is in the body or not, he cannot be said to be lifted up and rapt to that vision.[12]

The kind of vision which Moses demanded and got was the same as that which St. Paul called the "third heaven." It is the highest of three forms of vision, above sensation and above spiritual vision through corporeal images. It is a purely intellectual vision in which is seen the brightness of God, not through a corporeal or even spiritual figuration such as a meaningful image (*aenigma*) in a mirror, but face to face or, as Moses expressed it, mouth to mouth. This is the vision of God by that "species" by which God is what he is, however slightly the mind, even when purified of all corporeality, is able to grasp him. This is the same transcendent vision which St. Paul had and in which he saw, as we may well believe, the life in which we are to live forever.[13]

St. Augustine firmly and consistently taught that Moses and St. Paul, the two great parallel figures of the old and new dispensations, had both had a unique experience of God in seeing him as he is.[14] Whether or not St. Augustine had such a vision is open to question, and neither he nor St. Thomas, who accepts his authority in this matter, explicitly limits the experience to Paul and Moses.[15]

A passage from St. Augustine's *De quantitate animae* on the highest level of ascent of the soul to the divine describes what could easily be read as a direct intuition of the divine essence and alludes to a number of people who have had, and are still having, such an experience. The seventh and last level of the soul is the very vision and contemplation of Truth, a vision which brings an inexpressible joy and peace to the beholder. Great and incomparable souls who have actually seen and are seeing such things have disclosed this experience to the extent that they thought fitting. If we adhere to the course which God enjoins upon us, we shall by his power and wisdom come to the supreme Author of all things.[16]

Who were these great incomparable souls? Which men have seen and are still seeing the divine? Almost certainly St. Augustine means St. Paul and even, perhaps, Plotinus and Porphyry.[17] It is true that this work represents an earlier phase of St. Augustine's thought, but it is not anything he ever retracted, and in the absence of specific data to the contrary, we may assume that St. Augustine did not exclude the bare possibility of others sharing the experience of St. Paul and Moses.

The debate on this question continued, and in the twelfth century we find St. Bernard absolutely certain that no man in this life, neither a man of wisdom, nor a saint, nor a prophet, can have that direct vision of God, which is the prerogative of the blessed, and still be in this mortal flesh.[18] What is more, he specifically excludes Moses from such a vision, saying that Moses saw much less than he desired.[19] Still, St. Bernard did grant to St. Paul the highest mode of vision humanly possible. The lower forms of what St. Bernard calls "consideration" involve the use of the senses and things, either in the active or intellectual life. The highest form departs from the use of things and of the senses and, not by a graded ascent but by unexpected raptures, conducts us to the heights. Such was the rapture of Paul, and it was, as he tells us himself, a rapture and not an ascent, for he was caught up.[20]

The lower forms of consideration are nothing more than what we have called "speculation," seeing clearly the invisible things of God through the things that are made. The blessed, citizens of the true homeland, obviously have no need of such a ladder. The exiles, however, do have such a need. The higher form of consideration transcends creatures, sees more deeply into the things of heaven than is possible through the use of creatures. It sees the Word and the things made through the Word in the Word itself. It thus does not descend to things to get a knowledge of them, but sees them far better than in themselves. Consideration (of the highest kind) does not need the medium of the senses. It perceives immediately and is the best sort of vision. It satisfies the longing of the heart, and the person who has this capacity is content in himself.[21] There is thus, for St. Bernard, a form of rapture which leads to a most exalted and immediate knowledge of heavenly things, even the Word itself, but this is not —and this must be stressed—vision of God *per speciem*, however much St. Bernard may use the vocabulary of vision. On this matter he is abundantly clear, as we have seen even though some of his statements taken in isolation might seem to be capable of such an interpretation. We are often misled by the vocabulary of vision into thinking that "seeing," in mystical usage, necessarily means seeing *facie ad faciem*. But this is not so, and the great mystics were quite exact on this point.

This distinction will perhaps be made clearer if we turn to the writings of Richard of St. Victor, a famous contemporary of St. Bernard. Richard distinguished six kinds of contemplation: contemplation through the imagination alone, through the imagination but according to reason, "in the reason" but according to the imagination, "in the reason" but according to reason, above but not contrary to reason, and a last form of contemplation which is above reason and would seem to be beyond it.[22]

The sixth kind of contemplation meditates those things which are above reason and which seem to be beyond and even against reason. The soul exults and dances for joy when it has attained this supreme, most worthy, and lofty form of all the kinds of contemplation. Then it knows and contemplates by divine illumination all those things that human reason cries out against. Such things are virtually all the doctrines we are constrained to believe concerning the Trinity, which when considered in the light of human reason are no other than contradictory to it.[23] This is the form of contemplation which was experienced by St. Paul when he was rapt to the third heaven. It was a complete transcending of reason itself and arrives at the most contradictory of the articles of faith. St. Paul's rapture was the third and highest kind. The lowest merely rises above the corporeal senses; the next highest rises above the faculty of the imagination, a faculty which is a mean between the sensory and the rational.[24]

Yet, as we discover when we turn to Richard's *Mystical Annotations on the Psalms*, this highest form of contemplation just considered is not a vision of God in his essence. There are various modes of seeing God. We see him by faith when we firmly believe what is written in Scripture concerning him. We see him through contemplation when the truths of faith are imprinted on the eyes of our intelligence by divine inspiration, and we see him in his essence when he is seen as he is, in his own substance, face to face. Only the soul which has been assimilated to the divine nature can see him this way. Such an assimilation to the divine nature means an utter transcendence of the corporeal state, such as obtains in heaven, where God is eternally present and enjoyed and in the vision of whom there is rejoicing. God is said to dwell in a soul in this state.[25]

St. Thomas also takes up the question whether anyone in this life can see God *per essentiam*. It is, generally speaking, impossible, although he concedes that it happened in the case of Paul and Moses on the authority of St. Augustine. These occurrences, however, were out of the ordinary, although it has happened that the minds of some living in this flesh, but not employing the senses of the flesh, were raised to a vision of the divine essence, as St. Augustine says of both Moses and Paul. St. Thomas uses the phrase *mentes aliquorum*, which would seem to imply that he did not necessarily and explicitly confine the experience to the two great parallel figures, although one feels that he would have liked to. As will be seen, every time he treats the question he decides against the possibility of seeing the divine essence in this life but always makes an exception for the *Doctor Judaeorum* and the *Doctor gentium*.[26]

The contemplative life itself, the highest form of human activity, does not lead to a vision of the divine essence, unless as in the case of St. Paul the soul is freed from the necessity of using the organs of sense. His was, therefore, the supreme degree of contemplation possible in the present life and is a kind of mean between the eternal beatific vision after death and the kind of contemplative vision normally possible in this life.[27]

If contemplation never, or very infrequently and only by a special grace, attains to the divine substance, neither does prophecy. The prophetic vision is not a vision of the divine essence, nor do prophets see whatever they see in that essence. Their vision is through similitudes according to the degree of divine illumination that they receive. This kind of prophetic illumination may therefore be called a mirror, in that a mind so illumined contains a similitude of the truth of divine foreknowledge.[28] There are, however, grades of prophecy as there are grades of contemplation: that in which supernatural truth is received through imaginative visions, the middle grade in which supernatural truth is received without images, and the lowest form, which is also without images, but which receives truths of the human order intended to guide human relationships.[29] It was because Moses had seen God in his essence with the purest kind of intellectual vision that he is the greatest prophet of them all.[30]

St. Paul had seen the divine essence while still in this life, and his rapture was thus of the third and highest kind. The lowest form of rapture up to the contemplation of divine truth occurs through similitudes and through the imaginative faculty. Such, for example, was the rapture of St. Peter. The second form is the contemplation of divine truth through intelligible effects. Such was the experience of David. The third and highest kind, the kind experienced by St. Paul, was to see the divine essence. This is achieved through the "light of glory" and is permanently the prerogative of the blessed. It may also be experienced transitorily through a rapture; and such was the mode in which St. Paul experienced it while still in this life. The transitoriness of the experience makes the highest kind of rapture analogous to prophecy.[31]

The rapture of Paul took him beyond the outermost spheres to the empyrean or, if one agrees with John Damascene who does not believe in the existence of an empyrean, beyond the eighth sphere. There he saw those things which are entirely above corporeal nature. There he had a pure vision of intelligible things. This was the "third heaven" which he reached through a total alienation from the corporeal senses and from corporeal things. There he saw the intelligible universe as the angels and the blessed see it, and, even more, he saw

God in his essence. Thus, to go to the third heaven is to transcend the world of space and time, to enter the empyrean, and to have the beatific vision. It follows that anyone who goes beyond the last material confines of the universe in a rapture will have the beatific vision.[32]

Rapture is both an intellectual and an affective experience. From the point of view of the truth which is the goal of rapture it is, of course, intellectual. The efficient cause of the experience, however, may also be affective—the experience may begin from the desire for it. But since the person experiencing the rapture delights in his vision, even the intellectual goal has an affective aspect, involves both love and understanding. It was in order to point out this twofold aspect of the beatific vision that St. Paul described his rapture as both an ascent to the third heaven, which pertains to intellectual contemplation, and an ascent to paradise, which pertains to affect.[33] Rapture too is to be distinguished from ecstasy, for the former implies a certain violence in the departure from the self.[34]

Exactly what the status of contemplation and rapture is in the framework of St. Thomas' thought will be clearer if we examine his analysis of all the modes of knowing God. In question eighteen of *De veritate*, St. Thomas takes up the question of the knowledge of the first man in the state of innocence, and the first article is concerned with whether Adam in that state knew God through his essence. After considering the various aspects of the question St. Thomas decides that he did not, for he was still on the way to beatitude and had not achieved it.[35] Thomas explains that there are three modes of knowing God. After the fall we have need of a kind of mirror, in which there arises a likeness of God himself. For we can arrive at the invisible things of him only by the things that are made, according to Romans (1: 20).[36]

While man was still in a state of innocence, he did not need this sort of medium. He did, however, need a medium which is somewhat like the visible species of a thing, since he then saw God through a spiritual light which flowed from God into his mind and which was a kind of expressed likeness of the uncreated light.[37] In heaven, man will need neither a *speculum* nor a created *species* for seeing God, but the means of seeing him will be God's own essence. He will need no intelligible or sensible likeness of the Deity, for no such likeness can disclose God's essence. He will, however, need the light of glory and this will be a kind of medium by which God is seen, according to the Psalms (A.V. 36: 9): "In thy light we shall see light." The reason why this light of glory is needed is that this kind of truly supernatural sight is not natural to any creature, only to God, so that no creature can reach it by his own natural power but must be enlightened by a light from the divine.[38]

Contemplation is also a vision of God, but here he is seen through the medium of the light of wisdom. Although contemplation raises the mind to divine things, however, it does not rise to the immediate vision of the divine essence. In fact, it is not even as perfect a vision as Adam was capable of in the state of innocence.[39] This evaluation of contemplation is especially interesting in view of the fact that Dante's depiction of the "moment" of contemplation in the journey of the mind to God occurs, in the *Paradiso, after* he has been reconstituted in his unfallen human nature. The visions he receives after he has returned to the state of innocence in the garden of Eden are prophetic in character and would seem to correspond to that mode of prophecy effected through imaginative similitudes, a mode, as we have noted, that St. Thomas places below a purely intellectual kind of prophetic vision.

St. Thomas also makes some further elaborations of these modes of vision in discussing the rapture of St. Paul and whether he saw God in his essence. It would seem that he did not, for knowledge in this life of God is through a mirror or obscure but significative images (*aenigma*) of sensible creatures. The knowing of heaven, by which we see God in his essence, is natural only to God. Yet if this is so, it would go against the express authority of St. Augustine, for he says that St. Paul in his rapture did see God in his essence. But it is fitting that St. Paul should have had this vision, for it is not likely that such a vision would have been granted to Moses, the doctor of the Jews, and not to St. Paul, the doctor of the gentiles.[40] Here, on the authority of St. Augustine, St. Thomas assumes the authenticity of Moses' vision and argues for St. Paul's on the basis of the parallelisms of Old and New Testaments and the special revelations given to Jews and gentiles. Although St. Thomas usually defines vision *per speculum* as above, in at least one instance he seems to identify it with vision *per fidem*, with any indirect knowledge of God whether through creatures or through faith.[41] However, he usually reserves knowledge of God *per speculum* for the kind of knowledge which is gained through creation and which even a pagan could have.

Let us now turn to Dante, examine his allusions to St. Paul, and try to ascertain how he is related to this tradition of controversy over the nature of St. Paul's rapture and the kinds of knowledge of God that subsequent theologians derived from the Pauline texts we have considered. I will begin with the well-known passage from the letter to Can Grande della Scala where he explains his allusion to St. Paul in Canto I of the *Paradiso* and also refers to various famous contemplatives in support of his claim of having had some kind of supernatural vision:

And after he has said that he was in that place of Paradise which he describes by circumlocution, he goes on to say that he saw certain things which he who descends therefrom is powerless to relate. And he gives the reason, saying that "the intellect plunges itself to such depth" in its very longing, which is for God, "that the memory cannot follow." For the understanding of which it must be noted that the human intellect in this life, by reason of its connaturality and affinity to the separate intellectual substance, when in exaltation, reaches such a height of exaltation that after its return to itself memory fails, since it has transcended the range of human faculty. And this is conveyed to us by the Apostle where he says, addressing the Corinthians: "I know a man (whether in the body, or out of the body, I cannot tell; God knoweth) how that he was caught up to the third heaven, and heard unspeakable words, which it is not lawful for a man to utter." Behold, after the intellect had passed behind beyond the bounds of human faculty in its exaltation, it could not recall what took place outside of its range. This again is conveyed to us in Matthew, where we read that the three disciples fell on their faces, and record nothing thereafter, as though memory had failed them. And in Ezekiel it is written: "And when I saw it, I fell upon my face." And should these not satisfy the cavillers, let them read Richard of St. Victor in his book *On Contemplation;* let them read Bernard in his book *On Consideration;* let them read Augustine in his book *On the Capacity of the Soul;* and they will cease from their cavilling. But if on account of the sinfulness of the speaker they should cry out against his claim to have reached such a height of exaltation, let them read Daniel, where they will find that even Nebuchadnezzar by divine permission beheld certain things as a warning to sinners, and straightway forgot them. For He "who maketh his sun to shine on the good and on the evil, and sendeth rain on the just and on the unjust," sometimes in compassion for their conversion, sometimes in wrath for their chastisement, in greater or lesser measure, according as He wills, manifests his glory to evil-doers, be they never so evil.[42]

What strikes us most of all in this passage is Dante's identification of himself with St. Paul. As we have seen, whether or not St. Paul saw God in his essence, the fathers and doctors agreed that he achieved the highest form of supernatural vision possible in this life. He and Moses are the classic instances around which Christian mysticism focuses the discussion of its central problem of what exactly happens in the experience of contemplatives. Thus Dante's analogy between St. Paul and himself is intensely charged, and any theologically sophisticated reader of his time would have grasped the immensity of Dante's claim. Dante himself realizes it, for he immediately follows it up with a short list of mystical literature, the reading of which would stop all the cavilers and, by allusion to Nebuchadnezzar's brief illumination, enforces the point that you do not have to deserve such a vision to have it.

The question for us here is whether Dante was one of those who believed that St. Paul had seen God in his essence. If he did, then his claim is even more astounding, for the only two *certain* instances of such a vision in the theological literature were Moses and St. Paul. In the light of this question, the allusions he makes to Richard of St. Victor, St. Bernard, and St. Augustine are difficult to interpret. St. Paul is mentioned both in *De contemplatione*, as Dante calls the *Benjamin major*, and in *De consideratione*, as an example of one who experienced the highest form of mystical experience. In neither work is the question discussed whether he or any mortal can see God in his essence while still in this life, although both St. Bernard and Richard elsewhere decide against this possibility. Neither of them implies that St. Paul's rapture was singularly unique or virtually so. We must, however, bear in mind that the possibility of such an interpretation in either of these works is not excluded on the part of the reader, even if the authors would have rejected it. The vocabulary of mysticism is so involved with the terminology of spiritual vision, there is so much talk of seeing and understanding superrational truths such as the Trinity and Incarnation, that the texts could seem to be describing a vision of God's essence. As we have learned from our discussion of Richard of St. Victor, however, even seeing and understanding such mysteries does not mean seeing God "face to face."

St. Augustine in *De quantitate animae* does not mention St. Paul by name, but there is clearly a reference to him, along with a few unspecified others, as having seen the eternal truth. St. Augustine frequently used the vocabulary of vision in regard to the highest intellectual and intelligible things so that this work too could be read as saying that contemplatives see God's essence, something he was certainly willing to allow elsewhere to St. Paul and Moses if not to others.[43]

When we encounter these great contemplatives again in the *Paradiso*, what does Dante say of them? Richard appears in the heaven of the sun as one who in consideration was more than a man (*Par.* X, 131–132: "Riccardo / Che a considerar fu più che viro"); St. Augustine sits in the celestial rose of the empyrean (*Par.* XXXII, 35); and St. Bernard, Dante's final guide, is described merely as one who in our world tasted, through contemplation, of the peace of heaven (*Par.* XXXI, 110–111: "colui che 'n questo mondo, contemplando, gustò di quella pace"). I think it is significant that Dante does not say of St. Bernard that he saw heaven in this life, but simply that he had a taste of its peace, a way of describing a supernatural experience short of vision. As we shall see later, the only person Dante explicitly points out as having seen heaven is St. Paul.

In any case, the very least that Dante claims in the letter to Can Grande is an experience like St. Paul's, although we cannot determine from his claim in this instance how he conceives that experience. An examination of the references to St. Paul in the *Divine Comedy* will, I believe, elucidate his view of St. Paul's rapture and will throw light on one of the principles of structure of the work which is, in part, an imaginative representation and synthesis of all the Pauline modes of knowledge of God.

The first, and perhaps the most significant, mention of St. Paul occurs in the second canto of the *Inferno* when Dante learns from Virgil about the great journey he is to undertake (*Inf.* II, 10 ff.) through all the realms of the beyond. Dante is discouraged by what he feels is his weakness for the journey and awestruck at its magnitude. True, Aeneas, in the flesh, was granted a vision of the eternal world, but he had the universal mission of founding Rome and the Empire in preparation for the subsequent foundation of the Church. Analogously, St. Paul, the chosen vessel, went there to return with confirmation of the faith which is necessary for salvation. At this realization Dante feels so unworthy that he exclaims: "But I, why should I go there, and who grants it? I am not Aeneas; I am not Paul. Neither I nor any man thinks me fit for this, so that if I commit myself to go I fear lest my going be folly." [44]

Aeneas and St. Paul were the two men who, in the flesh, were granted universal visions necessary for their great missions. Indeed, Dante draws these two great figures even closer together by telling us that Aeneas heard things in his supernatural journey which were the cause of his victory (*Inf.* II, 26–27: "intese cose che furon cagione / di sua vittoria"), a phrase which suggests the *arcana verba* that St. Paul heard in his rapture, words which cannot be disclosed but which fitted him also for his mission. Of course, Dante the pilgrim is telling us that he is about to have a universal vision, a third one to be added to the two of Aeneas and St. Paul. But what is just as striking, if not as obvious, is that the great parallel to St. Paul in the tradition of mystical thought was not Aeneas but Moses and that Dante creates a new typology and parallelism of his own. The two consummate seers are not the *Doctor Judaeorum* and the *Doctor gentium* but the *pater Romanorum* and the *Doctor gentium.*

It is only when we see this passage in the light of the whole tradition of scriptural typological parallelism and mystical speculation that its force and boldness are made clear. The parallel between Moses and St. Paul was no more extrinsic and coincidental than the one between Adam and Christ as the second Adam. This is the way Providence governs history, each great figure in the drama of revelation being both a prophecy of what is to come and a pointing back to his archetype in what has been.

Dante very subtly takes up the Aeneas-Paul parallel again in *Paradiso* XV when he meets his ancestor Cacciaguida, a gem in the cross of souls in the heaven of Mars who leaves it to come to greet Dante. Cacciaguida reaches out "with such affection as Anchises showed to Aeneas when he recognized him in Elysium, if we may trust the account that Virgil, our greatest muse, gives." Cacciaguida then exclaims in Latin: "O my own blood! O grace of God poured forth above measure! To whom as to thee was heaven's gate ever opened twice?" [45]

The answer is obvious even though Dante does not give it. Such an experience was given to St. Paul. If Cacciaguida is, in Dante's private typology, an Anchises, then Dante is an Aeneas, but a celestial and Christian Aeneas, for the pagan real Aeneas is in limbo (*Inf.* IV, 122). The truly archetypal Christian Aeneas—again in Dante's private typology—is St. Paul. He is the Christian parallel, and to him, if to anyone, were the gates of heaven open twice, rapt while in this life to the highest heaven. What Dante here seems to be saying is that St. Paul received a unique vision shared by no other—except Dante himself. We have seen that where, in the mystical literature, St. Paul is singled out as truly unique it is in virtue of having seen God in his essence. Otherwise he is simply *primus inter pares,* not *primus super pares.* He certainly, in Dante's view, saw more than either Gregory or Dionysius, two great masters of contemplation (*Par.* XXVIII, 130–139), but I think that the implication of this passage is that St. Paul's vision was singular in some qualitative sense and not simply in degree, and the only qualitative difference there was which distinguished him from other mystics was that he saw God *facie ad faciem.* My interpretation of this episode will become clearer if we examine other Pauline allusions in the *Divine Comedy.*

The beginning of the rapturous ascent through the spheres of the *Paradiso* occurs when Dante looks upon the eyes of Beatrice after he is reconstituted in his truly human nature as God intended it to be before the Fall. At her aspect he was changed within, as Glaucus was after eating the herb which made him a sea-god. Dante now passes beyond the human condition at its most perfect, a condition greater than that which man enjoyed before the Fall (*Par.* I, 55 ff.). It is indescribable, and the example itself is really only for those to whom grace reserves the experience. Dante himself does not know, paraphrasing St. Paul, whether he was rapt in the spirit alone, that part which God created last, or in the flesh.[46]

When Dante enters the sphere of the moon, he again refers to his inability to know if he was in the body or not for, if he was, there must be interpenetration of substances, a thing which we cannot conceive. But this puzzle should only kindle our desire to see the essence of him in whom our nature was joined to God. For in the empyrean will be seen that which we hold by faith, not demonstrated but known *per se* like an axiomatic truth. In this episode we find not only a repetition of the reference to the famous text of St. Paul's in II Corinthians 12, but one to another text in the same letter where St. Paul draws the important distinction between walking by faith and by sight.[47]

That Pauline text, for later theologians, defined the difference between knowledge of God through faith and knowledge of his essence. This is certainly the meaning St. Augustine gave to it, and Dante agrees with him, for he speaks in this passage of how our eagerness to solve the puzzle of whether bodies interpenetrate kindles our desire to see the *essence.* (l. 41) of the Trinity in its aspect as the mystery of the Incarnation. This is precisely what Dante does see in the closing lines of the *Paradiso.* The double allusion to Paul and the reference to seeing the essence of God, a reference which turns out to be a promise which the poet as pilgrim fulfills, point unmistakably, in my opinion, to the conclusion that Dante was one of those who believed that St. Paul did see God in his essence.

The first twenty-nine cantos of the *Paradiso* are, in fact, an imaginative rendering of what it means to see God both *per fidem* and *per speculum* or *aenigma.* The ascent, in these cantos, takes place in space and time and is an ascent to the invisible things of God *a creatura mundi.* Persons, plants, things, all reflect the infinite eternal light in some finite mode. Simultaneously, we are enlightened concerning that body of dogma which constitutes the object of faith. The last four cantos are a rendering of seeing God *per speciem* or *facie ad faciem,* for to pass into the empyrean means nothing less than to see God in his essence. But before we examine the final vision let us turn to another allusion to St. Paul.

Dante and the Pauline Modes of Vision

In *Paradiso* XXVIII (100 ff.) Dante sees the angelic hierarchy as circles revolving around a point of minute intensity which is God. Beatrice explains their order, nature, and functions, and Dante uses this occasion to correct both the ordering he adopted in *Convivio* II, vi, derived from Isidore of Seville through Brunetto Latini, and the one put forth by Gregory. The true ordering is that of Dionysius, which differs from Isidore's in a shifting of Thrones, Dominations, Powers, and Principalities and from Gregory's in the interchange of Virtues and Principalities. Beatrice says:

And Dionysius set himself with such zeal to contemplate these orders that he named and distributed them as I do; but later Gregory differed from him, so that as soon as he opened his eyes in this heaven he smiled at himself. And if a mortal on earth set forth a truth so secret thou needst not marvel, for he that saw it here above revealed it to him, with much more of the truth of these circles.[48]

Dante here discusses three of the greatest mystics he knew and orders them according to clarity of vision, with St. Paul at the top followed by Dionysius and Gregory. It is clear that Dionysius, through amorous contemplation, was able to order the angelic hierarchy correctly, yet Dante also says that he was able to divulge such a secret truth because St. Paul told him about it. These two statements would seem to be contradictory unless we assume that whatever contemplative vision Dionysius possessed needed to be verified to him by St. Paul. It is clear that St. Gregory was mistaken, and he was, let us recall, a great medieval authority on the contemplative life. St. Gregory's error is especially significant in view of his insistence on the impossibility of seeing eternal things, especially God, clearly and his frequent use of "fog" and "cloud" to qualify the degree of contemplative vision.

Dante, in effect, allows to Gregory precisely the kind of contemplative vision Gregory thought possible. Similarly with Pseudo-Dionysius, who frequently refers to St. Paul as his *manuductor* (*cheiragogos*), or instructor.[49] He is therefore given a lesser and apparently indirect knowledge of the angelic hierarchy. What is certainly clear is that Paul is singled out as the greatest visionary, as the man who really saw heavenly things as they are.

Whether or not Dante the man had a vision of God's essence in the mortal state is really a meaningless question. But that Dante as author of and character in the *Divine Comedy* claims and describes such a vision is beyond doubt. Dante the pilgrim is in heaven, so that he is committed in terms of the universe of the poem to the rendering of such a vision, and Dante the author of the letter to Can Grande, commenting on the final part of his poem, presents a claim which, taken together with those of the *Comedy*, insists on the reality of the vision the pilgrim sees. The final rapturous visions of God's essence in the *Paradiso* are given to us as *remembered* by the author of the poem.

Dante prepares us for this final vision in *Paradiso* XXX by his description of his acquisition of a new sense of sight, a *novella vista*, a sight so strong that it will bear any light, even that essential, immaterial light of God.[50] The pilgrim in order to complete his journey must acquire a new kind of vision whereby he sees with the eyes of the soul or mind, a vision whereby invisible and intelligible things are seen in their essence and immediately.[51] Dante magnificently describes for us the gradually developing powers of this new sense of sight, its first visions through images which gradually are replaced with their realities. Paradise first appears as a river of light from which emerge living sparks, but after Dante drinks with his eyes from that river, he sees both the courts of paradise made plain. His growing vision so excites him that he begins to repeat some form of the verb "to see" every few lines, especially *vidi*, "I saw," on which he makes a triple rhyme.[52]

The next two cantos are devoted to the growth of his newly acquired powers, his transfer from Beatrice to St. Bernard, and, most important, his prayer to the Virgin for that final grace necessary to have the beatific vision. Upon conclusion of the prayer, Dante's sight became even purer and began entering more deeply into the exalted light which is true *in itself*, not the light which simply makes truth in finite intellects (*Par.* XXXIII, 52–54: "chè la mia vista, venendo sincera, / e più e più intrava per lo raggio / dell'alta luce che da sè è vera"). Then, in a passage of surpassing power, Dante completely reverts to his role as narrator of what the pilgrim experienced:

From that moment my vision was greater than our speech, which fails at such a sight, and memory too fails at such excess. Like him that sees in a dream and after the dream the passion wrought by it remains and the rest returns not to his mind, such am I; for my vision almost wholly fades, and still there drops within my heart the sweetness that was born of it. Thus the snow loses its imprint in the sun; thus in the wind on the light leaves the Sibyl's oracle was lost.[53]

This residue of his great experience is like the imprinted passion of a dream, the feeling of joy which remains upon awakening but without the content, which has fled. His memory too fails at such a sight, and this memory is not what we ordinarily mean by memory, but what St. Augustine calls a "loving memory," the only thing he carried back with him when his mind was carried up, in the flash of a twinkling eyesight, to the sight of that which *is*, to the invisible things of God which are understood by the things that are made.

This "loving memory," the residue of his vision of ultimate truth, is an appetite for what he had smelled, but had not been able to eat of.[54]

St. Augustine's memory is similar to, but not really like, the platonic *anamnesis*, the unconscious retention of things seen in some early, disembodied existence. It is rather that portion of man's spirit which is the seat of both self-consciousness and self-transcendence, that place in which all men retain their implicit awareness of God's existence and in which the contemplative guards the residue, the "loving memory," of his vision of that which truly is.[55] It is that partial knowledge of God which presupposes the human quest of him, and it is what remains if the quest is successful in this life. What Dante is able to recall from this memory is the final vision in its final form, purged of the imagery of speculation and the less exalted forms of contemplation. It is the vision of the reality toward which all the earlier images of the *Paradiso* pointed.

Dante first has a sight of God as essential light, as a living ray, which is so keen that he would have been dazzled if he turned away, although he is able to sustain it and determines to continue to do so until he attains the infinite goodness.

I think, from the keenness I endured of the living ray, that I should have been dazzled if my eyes had been turned from it; and I remember that for this cause I was the bolder to sustain it until I reached with my gaze the Infinite Goodness.[56]

The last clause of this passage also translates "so that I reached the infinite goodness with my glance or face." It is thus at this moment that Dante begins his rendering of a sight of God *facie ad faciem*, and the first essential attribute of God that he sees is God as the Good, as *summum bonum*.

Dante then looks into the essential light which is God,

enabled to do so by the abundance of grace which he now possesses. He next sees, in its depths, substance and accidents and their relationships, the categories of reality in their transcendent uncreated being, fused in such a unified way that they appear to be a simple light. He believes that he saw the universal form of this great knot of categories because he feels his joy expand, he experiences a growing vividness of that "loving memory" of his vision.[57] The universal form of the categories in their transcendent reality is nothing more than uncreated being itself, God's essence. The simple light into which being is fused is another essential attribute of God, his unity. Dante then returns to his vision of God as the Good when he tells us that it is a light the sight of which makes it impossible for anyone ever to fix his gaze on anything else, since all the good which is the object of the will is gathered up in that final good's perfection.[58]

God has so far been seen as *summum verum*, the light which in itself is true, *summum bonum et summum unum*, supreme goodness and unity, and as *summum ens*, that kind of being whose essence is its existence. But this is still the God of the philosophers, not the God of the Christians, and the rest of the canto is taken up with Dante's magnificent rendering of his vision of the Trinity, the direct intuition of a paradox. It first appears as three concentric circles, and upon further gaze the human likeness of the Incarnate Deity appears within the circlings (XXXIII, 115–136). Dante then wanted to see how the image is fitted to the circle, but his own wings were not sufficient for that. Suddenly he was struck by a flash and his mind received its wish; his desire and will, infinitely satisfied, took on the circular motion of eternal spirit in harmony with "the Love that moves the sun and other stars." [59]

Dante thus recapitulates all of the Pauline modes of knowledge and experience of God. He is seen *per speculum* and *facie ad faciem, per fidem* and *per speciem.* We ascend to a sight of the *invisibilia ipsius a creatura mundi,* and through the power of the poet's imagination we become that man, Dante or St. Paul, *raptus usque ad tertium coelum, in paradisum.* God is seen as supreme light, being, unity, and truth and above all as the Trinity enclosing the mystery of the Incarnation. The final flash is the perfect understanding of this mystery, a truth which Dante cannot remember although he has seen and understood it, a truth which is the essence of the Christian God and which completes all possible human knowledge of him either in this life or in the hereafter.[60]

The rendering of the beatific vision, the crucial allusions to St. Paul as well as the identification that Dante makes with him, all indicate not only that the universe of the *Paradiso* is an imaginative rendering and synthesis of the Pauline modes of vision, but that Dante included among those visions seeing God in his essence. Dante's work has often been called vision literature, and it obviously ought to be. The important point is that Dante worked in a tradition which made elaborate distinctions between kinds of vision—direct and indirect, prophetic and contemplative, apocalyptic and rapturous—and that his journey in one important aspect is a journey through higher and higher modes as well as degrees of vision. Studies of Dante in relation to this tradition may offer new insights into the principles of structure which govern the universe of the *Divine Comedy*.[61]

V

Plato's "Eros" and Dante's "Amore"

BOTH Dante and Plato inherited from the past a complex of attitudes, legends, and literature about love, and in both cases it was a special kind of love, love as an ennobling passion. Plato confronted the problem of so-called Dorian love, imported into cultured Attica from the Dorian regions of Greece where it had formed part of the ethos of a warrior class. It soon became a widespread practice, and in its most refined form it was conceived of as a passion which made the warrior brave and engendered civic as well as military virtues. The stories of Harmodius and Aristogeiton, Cratinus

and Aristodemus, the later versions of the friendship of
Achilles and Patroclus, all testify to the military and civic
heroism which was believed to emerge from this form of
masculine affection.

Dante inherited a heterosexual form of ennobling love,
chivalric and courtly in tone, which engendered virtues in
the lover similar to those produced by Greek love. It made
the knight brave in battle, courteous and gentle to the weak,
and resolute as a champion of justice. In both platonic and
chivalric love, the lover was filled with a kind of "irrational"
impulse, *mania* or *joie*, the impulse to ennoblement.

These loves, which in their highest forms were chaste, were
closely bound to moral and social evils, to pederasty in the
one case and to adultery in the other.[1] They were thus involved with vices which were really distortions of their highest ideals, and what appeared as ennoblement easily became
degradation. In addition, both of these codes were importa-
tions from military aristocracies into societies of tradesmen,
thinkers, and artists. They were not organic either to the
Athenian *polis* or the Florentine *commune*. In either case
the code had an "alien" quality—it demanded some kind of
adaptation on the part of the societies which were trying to
assimilate them. Neither the Athenians nor the Florentines
could accept a code simply as a code. It had to be understood
and imagined, its good and bad elements distinguished; it had,
in short, to be given a meaning.

The legends of lovers in classical antiquity, the Provençal
lyrics, the tractates of love such as Andreas' *De amore*, were
not only inconsistent in the ideals they represented, but were
simply representations of attitudes of *gesta amoris*, deeds accomplished through the power of love, lacking in conceptual
content and essentially unintelligible to the speculative intel-

lect. It was the work of Plato, and of Dante and some of his predecessors, to conceptualize, refine, and formulate the codes of love they inherited. They not only tried to render these codes intelligible but tried as well to give a moral direction to a passion which could create value but which often corrupted. From one point of view, Dante and Plato can be seen as culminators and synthesizers of a tradition. They arrive at their respective positions by both criticizing their predecessors and assimilating what they felt was positive in what they criticized.

Love is a constant theme in the work of Dante from the early visions of the *Vita nuova* to the final ecstasy of the *Paradiso*. It appears in all of its many forms, personal and cosmological, natural and supernatural, human and divine. What interests us most, however, in our confrontation of Dante and Plato is the peculiar union of personal and particular love with some transcendent love which contains it. The Dante-Beatrice relationship in the *Vita nuova* and the *Comedy* reveals, as it develops and changes, the universalization of the particular, the eternalization of the temporal. From this point of view, the *Paradiso* is the truly platonic moment of Dante's universe, for here we see the beloved doing her saving work through her ever-increasing beauty, luring Dante, through love, up the ladder of light and beauty to the threshold of absolute reality and, having fulfilled her purpose, leaving him to other agencies to finish his journey.

Although the *Paradiso* is the great synthesis of creative loves, the nature of Dante's achievement in that section might be better understood if his view of love in the *Convivio* is examined. That inconsistent and puzzling work is in part the rough draft of many of the ideas and attitudes found clustering around the figure of Beatrice, although there they are applied to "lady philosophy," the abstraction Dante made of the apparently concrete figure of the *donna gentile* of the *Vita nuova*.

In the third book of the *Convivio* (ii, 3) Dante calls love the spiritual union of the soul and the loved thing. It is, to be more precise, the *virtus unitiva*, the power which unites the person with an object which appears to it as beautiful or good. Dante explains that the soul is of divine origin, its existence has a divine source, and it seeks to fortify its own existence by union with God and with the divine excellences manifested in nature, the power of love being more intense as the divine excellences appear more perfect (ii, 5 ff.). These divine excellences are actually finite and particular manifestations of the Divinity, mirror images or *specula* which reflect in part the infinite, divine light which is God. Indeed, the whole created universe is no more than a collection of such "mirrors" or, as St. Bonaventura would have said, of "footprints" (*vestigia*) of God.

These reflections of divine attributes are not, however, all of the same kind or of the same intensity. They constitute a hierarchy of mounting luminousness, beauty, being, excellence, and goodness, the more so as they are nearer to their Creator. Corresponding to this ladder of creation, there exists a ladder of love, a love which increases with the excellence of its object and is ultimately a desire for God or Wisdom. It is what one loves on this scale of objects that, Dante tells us, permits us to recognize the quality of a person's soul, the inner quality being revealed through the outer things it loves (ii, 9).

Dante proceeds in the next chapter of this book (iii) to a consideration of the kinds and degrees of love. All levels of creation from the mineral, through the vegetable and animal, up to the rational have their own kind of love, their own inner tendency to fulfill their place and function in the universe. Man who shares in all these natures is a microcosm of loves. His gravity, his attachment to the time and place of his generation, his appetite for nutritious food, his desires for the pleasure of the senses, and his desire for truth and virtue constitute a hierarchy of the kinds of love that inhere in his composite nature.

Later on, in Book IV, Dante returned to the nature of love in man and set these various loves in a dialectical and dynamic relationship to one another (xii, 16–18). There he tells us that since the soul had its origin in God it is impelled, through the loves of which it is capable, to return to him. It turns when it is young to objects of appetite such as an apple, then as it grows older to various objects of the sensible faculties such as a little bird, clothing, and a woman. Then it seeks riches in greater and greater quantity, testing each thing in turn and always disappointed because it can find only in God what it really seeks.

The *donna gentile* revealed much of the divine light; she was in the order of manifestations of divinity high up the ladder. Her beauty was of such an order that language and thought cannot express or understand all that is true concerning her. This inability to comprehend her is of the same kind as one might experience in trying to understand spiritual substances. In such a case the mind is, as it were, transparent to the illuminating ray of truth and cannot arrest it (III, ii, iv). To this intensity of beauty there corresponds an equal intensity of love. Indeed, the desire for the *donna gentile*—or allegorically the Wisdom of God—cannot be sated on earth (vi).

As a personification, she is also the prototype in the mind of God of perfect humanity, the best human person possible, and God endowed her with more of his excellence than is

properly due to human nature. Her soul, supereminently endowed by God with perfection, infuses its virtue into her
body revealing, *as beauty*, something of the excellence of
God who made it. The resultant bodily beauty reveals won-
derful things and arouses longings to behold and contemplate
them. The sensible beauty of the body is thus a translation
of the beauty of the soul which is in turn a revelation or manifestation of the beauty of God. This human beauty, fundamentally spiritual but also manifesting itself through sensible
particulars, is an especially revealing *speculum* and arouses
powerful desires in the beholder. But these desires are not
sensual; they reach for a beauty which lies deep in the heart
of things and which, in God, turns to truth.

The beauty of the lady philosophy is thus of a miraculous
kind and, since it is a finite mirror image of infinite beauty,
it aids our faith (vii). In this respect it is a foretaste of heavenly bliss, and the beauty of her eyes and smile are adorn-
ments placed there by a special act of the universal principle
of love which guides all things to the place that they belong
(viii). The eyes and smile are thus divine lures. The most
beautiful parts of the body, they therefore have in the highest degree the power to arouse desire and to guide the beholder to the heavenly "place" in which his existence is
rooted. The sensible aspect of the *donna gentile* reveals something of the pleasures of paradise, although not as in paradise,
for joy is uninterrupted there. Her beauty has not only a
revealing power but a saving power in that it can make a new
nature in those who gaze upon it (viii). The wondrous things
which sensible beauty reveals thus point to a fulfillment in
paradise, a fulfillment beyond the grave in an eternal enjoy-
ment of the delights of beauty. The longings which she
arouses are thus "holy longings."

So far in discussing his ode "Love, that discourses to

me in my mind," Dante has focused his commentary on the literal level. This level describes a paragon of beauty and the effects of that beauty on the beholder. The *donna gentile* of the literal level becomes "lady philosophy" on the allegorical level, and Dante's commentary then focuses on the beauties and powers of philosophy. True philosophy must have both love and zeal, and the whole of chapter xi of Book III of the *Convivio* is devoted to a consideration of the necessity of love in the pursuit of wisdom. Philosophy as a personal acquisition cannot come into being without a passion for ideas, a desire to know with true zeal, a zeal which sustains the thinker in his quest for truth (xi, 8–12). Indeed, the love of truth is the efficient cause of philosophy. Philosophy is no more than the loving exercise of that true wisdom which exists supremely in God as Highest Wisdom, Love, and actuality (xii, 12–13). It is, so to speak, a species of the genus love, and love is its absolute presupposition. The exiled angels cannot philosophize precisely because love is absent in them (xiii, 2).

As God attracts us through the sensible beauty of the *donna gentile*, so he also attracts us by the *beauty* of philosophy, ennobling our natures and making them beautiful and virtuous (xiii, 9). Love is the very form of philosophy, and her matter is wisdom (xii, 1–12). Her demonstrations and persuasions, the most beautiful things about her, are her eyes and her smile, and, like the physical eyes and smile of sensible beauty, they reveal the joys of paradise. As the smile of the beautiful lady translates the inner light of the soul as beauty, the smile of philosophy translates the inner light of wisdom as through a veil (xv, 2). The beauty of philosophy is morality, the ordering of the virtues, as the beauty of the body results from an ordering of parts (xv, 11–12). Thus the beauty of philosophy is analogous to the perfect beauty of the perfect individual of the species in that it cannot be defined and even exceeds the powers of intellect to comprehend (xv, 6; viii, 15).

Throughout the whole of Book III, the commentary on the *canzone* "Love that discourses to me in my mind," there is a perplexing shift of emphasis. We are told on the one hand that the lady of Dante's love is primarily divine wisdom. We are also told that she is the wisdom of the angels and of men as well as the various sciences constituting, collectively, human wisdom. On the other hand, Dante personifies philosophy as the most perfect female specimen of the human species, so perfect that she is virtually an angel. Dante consequently shifts his point of view, in what appears to be an inconsistent manner, from the lover of a person to a lover of wisdom and knowledge. This inconsistency is further compounded when we discover a third conception of the *donna pietosa* as the archetype of humanity as it exists in the divine mind: she is the divine intention or form in respect to mankind. This conception lies midway between the literal meaning of the lady as the perfect human being and the allegorical rendering of her as divine wisdom. Thus the focus of the commentary shifts, going from the consideration of various kinds of wisdom, to knowledge, to the divine archetype of humanity, to a human being of perfect grace and beauty.

These several elements or meanings of the lady of the ode are also present in Beatrice, but in a more unified and consistent manner. In the *Comedy*, Beatrice has completely assumed all the qualities of the *donna pietosa* of the *Convivio*. I can offer nothing new in a biographical way on the question of the riddle of the *donna gentile* and on the precise nature of Dante's betrayal of and return to Beatrice. With the data at hand we are reduced to conjecture. Prescinding from biographical considerations, however, we can examine the inconsistencies in Dante's treatment of the lady of the ode in terms of the theory of allegorical interpretation he advances at the beginning of Book II.

Dante there maintains that one of the differences between theological allegory and poetic allegory is that the former may be true in both the literal and allegorical meanings whereas the latter is true only in the allegorical sense. The poet invents stories out of his own head, and they can thus be considered only as beautiful lies meant, however, to refer to some truth of a moral nature. There is thus a tendency for the allegorical level to cancel out the literal level, for the truth lies in the former alone. This tendency works against another one, that of having the allegorical meaning complete the literal meaning. I think that the problem of poetic truth conceived as the problem of allegory presented Dante with the choice of "either/or" when what he seemed to want in his actual commentary was "both."

There are times in his commentary when he discusses physical beauty in a person—whether an actual person or an imaginary one is not here important—and other times when this actual consideration of physical beauty is treated as a metaphor for the immaterial beauty of wisdom. The lover (literal level) and the philosopher (allegorical level) and the corresponding objects of their love, perfect human beauty and wisdom, are on different planes. The levels of meaning are presented to us as negating one other, and simultaneously we are aware of Dante's attempt to have them complete each other. This contradiction is the result of Dante's not having thought out a harmonious relationship between love of beauty in a person and love of the beauty of divine wisdom. His conception of the lady as the divine idea of humanity apparently is an attempt to mediate these extremes.

Beatrice as found in the *Comedy* is the result of a successful synthesis of these various ideas: a concrete person of surpassing beauty, the beloved of the First Lover whose beauty surpasses anything seen on earth and who therefore most fully embodies her "idea," and the lure which leads the lover through the ladder of reality to the beauty of the divine wisdom. We might thus say that Beatrice mediates the "allegorical" and "literal" levels by going from one to the other in her death, by assuming a greater immaterial beauty in lieu of her corporeal beauty, great as that was. Personal corporeal beauty passes over into a greater immaterial beauty and, in so doing, increases the lover's ardor and leads him through the universe, which is the very object and content of philosophy, to the threshold of the highest grace itself.

From this point of view, Dante's great confession on the summit of Purgatory is a confession of having betrayed the God of love. I again prescind from biographical considerations as to whether the "false loves" of Dante's period of error were carnal or intellectual or both, whether the *donna gentile* was an actual person whom he loved or simply an ideal creation. We do not know if Dante's error was to love philosophy too much or another woman too much or both too much. One thing, however, is clear: he should have continued to love Beatrice more after her death, and, if he had continued to pursue with his enamored mind her greater beauty, he would not have fallen into error.

The sin was a sin against the God of love because it was a sin against the *ordering of love*. He may have loved something base or even something fine or noble in the wrong way, or he may have loved a succession or a plurality of things in an improper way. Dante does not tell us and he did not intend to, for the ideal date of the *Comedy* is 1300 and all the events he wishes to reveal from a lifetime of experience are compressed into a week and imbedded in a fiction. The events of the *Convivio*, if it is the record of a period of error, could not have happened much earlier than 1308, but they are atoned for in the *Comedy* by the ideal date of 1300. The pattern of the *Vita nuova*, written no later than 1295, is consistent with the scheme of the *Comedy*, but the *Convivio* is not. Was there a second draft of the *Vita nuova* which established this harmony? If so there isn't a shred of textual evidence for this view anywhere. The attempt to elicit Dante's biography from his works, especially the *Comedy*, is to fail to realize that the biographical elements in the poem are eternalized, rendered timeless, selected for the moral lessons which they may have for humanity and by a criterion which considers their ultimate significance and not their immediate and literal reality.

The elements of the platonic doctrines of love, it is clear, were all present in the *Convivio* but were not fully worked out. The connection between the joys of paradise which the lady revealed here and those joys *there* was not fully understood. Dante knew that the Wisdom which lies at the origin of the world "changes" to beauty, indeed is beauty. What he had to discover was that Beatrice could guide him to that goal, and how and why she could. In the *Comedy*, the lover-poet and philosopher are unified in the one individual who makes the journey. As Beatrice grows lovelier and lovelier, Dante grows wiser and wiser and more and more amorous. Love of beauty and love of wisdom are one; they do not tend to negate each other but operate harmoniously on every level in the soul's journey to God.

These doctrines and attitudes of Dante's that we have been considering bear a striking resemblance to some of the most important ideas in Plato's *Phaedrus* and *Symposium*.[2] An examination of Plato's ideas is therefore in order before we continue our study of Dante's conception of love. In the

Phaedrus (250D) Plato tells us that eyesight is the sharpest, most singular of the senses and that its purpose is, by perceiving corporeal beauty, to awaken a desire for the greater incorporeal form of beauty.[3] This awakening of desire for immaterial beauty is a kind of recollection. In an original pre-existent state, when the soul followed the train of the gods in its winged flight through the heavens, it saw all the perfect and glorious forms of Absolute Beauty, Justice, Wisdom, and Sophrosyne. None of the souls, however, have the full vision of these forms and do not pass beyond the heavens to the "plain of truth" itself, although some souls see more than others (248A-B). The souls finally fall and are incarnated in the various kinds of men—from philosopher down to tyrant—depending on how much of the plain of truth they were able to see. Only one of all the forms seen while the soul flew along the underside of the heavens is now visible, beauty. The other forms such as justice are barely perceptible and only to "dull organs," the rational faculties.

When the souls of men fell from the heavens, they forgot what they had seen, partly because of the imperfections of their vision in the pre-existent state and partly because of evil associations in their present incarnations.[4] The vision of corporeal beauty reminds them of the greater beauty seen and forgotten, indeed it is the function of corporeal beauty to induce *anamnesis* (250D) and to regrow the wings which the soul lost in the collisions brought about by the difficulty of the charioteer in controlling the "dark horse" of the soul.

Reminded by corporeal beauty of perfect beauty, the soul is fired with a nostalgic, irresistible longing to recapture it. This experience is a transport, a supernatural obsession, the divine power of Eros which possesses the soul and goads it into ascending to beauty itself (250D–252C). This possession is a form of divine madness or *mania*, akin to the divine

madness of the prophet, the poet, and the theurge, and constitutes a fourth type of madness, that of the lover. The
poet who is "mad" or *entheos* is to be carefully distinguished
from the poet who occupies a rather low place, the sixth, in
the order of incarnations and who is a mere "imitative" artist.
The poet who is "mad" is the instrument of a divine "educa-
tion" (*paideia*), the glorifier of the countless mighty deeds of
ancient times for the instruction of posterity. He is inspired
and a follower of the muses (*mousikos*). There are therefore
two kinds of poets as there are two kinds of prophets, those
with and those without divine madness, which is as superior
to human sanity as the poetry of madness is to the "poetry of
skill" (245A–248E).[5]

The power man has to think conceptually and philosophically is the result of his reminiscence of the forms which he
beheld in the divine procession (249B-C). Thus the philosopher naturally occupies the first place in the order of possible
incarnations the soul takes after it falls from the divine procession. But the philosopher is also joined as an equal to the
lover of beauty, the lover, and the follower of the muses
(248D, *philosophos, philokalos, erotikos, mousikos*).

From one point of view, these four types are not four persons distinct from one another, but actually are four different "qualities" of one activity. The *philokalos, mousikos,*
and *erotikos* are not persons other than the *philosophos* but
denote aspects of him. The terms "lover of beauty" and "follower of the muses" are the two which are virtually synonymous, and "lover" and "lover of wisdom" indicate respectively the erotic-creative and intellectual moments of
philosophical activity.

On the other hand, the four types are distinguishable
and can be considered examples of separate ways of reach-
ing the same reality. The lover of beauty "knows" the same

ultimate reality known by the lover of wisdom, for in the pre-existent state they shared in the same vision of the moral forms of which beauty and truth are, as it were, co-ordinate species. Whether a man is described primarily as a lover, philosopher, lover of beauty, or follower of the muses depends on the quality or character of his striving after the absolute reality which he is trying to recapture. Every "striver" has something of each quality in his striving, but one predominates. All Eros involves the passionate pursuit of the truly real through beauty, wisdom, and knowledge or the arts of the muses.

In its previous life, the soul simply *saw* all the moral forms directly. In its incarnation it dimly *thinks* some of them and *sees* one in a complete embodiment—beauty. Unlike justice, beauty is as fully manifested in the world of space and time as any moral form can be. We know that there can be more truth and more justice, but "a thing of beauty is a joy forever." That is why its effect is overpowering and starts the "knowing-amorousness" or "amorous-knowing" which compels us up a ladder of beauty, a ladder whose nature is described in the *Symposium* (210A).

There, the scale of beautiful forms goes from beauty of bodies to beauty of souls, to beauty of laws and traditions, to beauty of sciences, and to the science which is knowledge of beauty. The final step is to reach supreme being, the highest intelligible reality as *the object of love*. This love is, as we have seen, a *mania* whose source is the "plain of truth," a nonrational emotion which is later joined to and governed by reason, a "madness" which finds its highest fulfillment in the philosophic vision. Eros is thus a kind of interpreter, a messenger or mediator between the soul and ultimate reality, and he enters through the eyes.

The entry of Eros through the eyes reminds us of the

peculiar importance of the whole apparatus of vision in Plato's thought. There was for him an intrinsic analogy between the nature of physical vision and intellectual vision, between the eyes of the body and the eyes of the soul. Similarly, there was an important correspondence between the light of the sun of the intelligible world, the Good, and the light of its offspring, the physical sun.[6] The ascent from the sensible to the intelligible through a ladder of beauty implies the transition from a physical sense to a spiritual sense. Thus, Eros may enter through the physical eyes, but it initiates a process which brings the eyes of the soul into play.

Eros operates the way it does because it is fundamentally a desire for the *everlasting* possession of the Good, the impulse toward immortality (204D, 206E). The Good which the soul seeks is also the Beautiful, which from Plato down to the eighteenth century was considered an aspect of the Good (201C). But both the lover of wisdom and the lover of beauty are incapable of remaining satisfied for long with the object of their desire and are possessed by a divinely inspired discontent by which "the resources he gets will ever be ebbing away" and he must therefore continually ascend the ladder of beauty (203E).

Beauty presents itself in a series of higher and higher manifestations, and the vision of beauty leads to a "procreation" followed by a desire for a fresh and higher beauty. In this process the intellect (*nous*) plays an important part, for it discerns the one in the many and makes generalizations and identifications (210B-C). Indeed, Eros is the philosophic impulse itself, the very "love of ideas." In its aspect as mean between wisdom and ignorance, Eros is the philosopher himself whose knowing lies in the fact that he is aware of his "unknowing" (cf. *Symposium* 203D ff.).

Beauty, however, is also bound to knowledge (210C), and

the love of knowledge in its procreative phase is the sphere of production of beautiful thoughts (*kaloi logoi*) occasioned by the sight of the great sea of beauty (210A ff.). The true lover's life is a journey, an ascent from the particular and corruptible beauties of sense to the general and more permanent beauties of mind.

To prophetic temperaments like Dante and Plato, passion and reason, cognition and feeling, are blended. This blending generates the kind of religious emotion characteristic of both—a holy awe before the vision of beauty, an intellectual passion which is essentially expansive and propagative, overflowing into a creative activity which is at the same time philosophic, artistic, prophetic, and "amorous."

This amorousness is not to be interpreted in the light of modern doctrines of sublimation. Plato, like Dante, regards the highest forms of desire as primary. For Plato, the lower forms are found in those grades of being which the soul experiences when incarnate. Sexual desire is thus only the lowest form of the passion for immortality, "an accidental appanage of existence in time." [7] It is the lowest analogue of an impulse which finds successively higher objects, such as the pursuit of fame, which will survive the death of the individual, and the pursuit of wisdom through philosophy. It is fundamentally the means by which the soul recovers its divine nature.

The inmost desire of the divine part of the soul, its desire for immortality, can be satisfied by the pursuit of wisdom. This divine part is truly a guiding genius lifting us from earth to heaven "like a plant whose roots are not in earth but in the heavens" where it first came to birth (*Timaeus*, 90A).

Thus although Eros in the narrow sense is the sexual impulse, in the larger sense it appears as all striving toward value. Spiritual striving and carnal striving can be classified together not only because they are both species of the genus "striving" but because sexual Eros is the initial vehicle of spiritual "soaring." Sexual Eros cannot remain fixed in a beautiful body or soul, for the condition of being beautiful is common to all things that Eros governs, and beauty is simply that which awakens and channels the erotic-creative impulse.[8]

The lover who pursues beauty through its graded manifestations in the sexual rhythm of desire-procreation-fresh desire finally reaches the idea of the beautiful. When he reaches this, he finds that he has also reached the Good and True and thereby participates in the highest knowledge and virtue. Truth, Beauty, Goodness, constitute a unity in the absolutely real so that the philosopher and lover may reach the same goal through different paths.

The *Symposium* and the *Phaedrus* present us with two complementary aspects of love, both of which are present in later speculation on love and in Dante. In the *Symposium*, love is conceived as a progress through a hierarchically ordered reality so that love is personified as a *daemon*, a mediator between gods and men. In the *Phaedrus*, love is a kind of possession so that it is personified as a god or something divine—not merely as a mediatory *daemon*. Love is thus a progress from want to satisfaction, misery to bliss, ignorance to knowledge; but it is also a kind of divine rapture in which a god fills the worshiper with a supernatural and superrational power.

Dante's ladder of beauty as light and the platonic ladder of beautiful forms both turn into a ladder of love, of a love which beauty engenders. This beauty is a reflection, an embodiment or manifestation of absolute beauty, and the love it engenders must therefore rise to the source of beauty. The question arises as to the function of the person in this ladder. We have seen that all creatures in their various ways and degrees reflect this absolute beauty in some finite mode, and so does man.[9] Even where Dante's contemporaries and predecessors considered the human body one of the noblest corporeal manifestations of beauty, they admired human beauty in a universal way. They speculated on the beauty of "human bodyness" rather than the beauty of any particular individual. Dante himself, in the *Convivio*, tends to treat human beauty in a generalized way and shifts from a generic to a particular consideration of the subject in an apparently inconsistent manner.

When Beatrice is finally reasserted, however, we have a true reconstitution of the *Phaedrus* doctrine. It is the presence of a concrete individual in the ladder of love and beauty that is the true note of the platonic doctrine of love. A beautiful person initiates the erotic flight to the supreme reality. Dante differs from Plato in that for him the *mania* of the poet and that of the lover are one. Plato thought that the inspired poet and the lover are in contact with the plain of truth through two different or distinguishable kinds of the four kinds of *mania*. For Dante, however, the lover and the poet rise as one, through love, to God. In either case the goal is the same. The lover of beauty, the follower of the muses, the lover of wisdom, and the "erotic" lover all meet in ultimate reality where a unique vision transcends and replaces both physical sight and the capacities of ordinary human thought.

This erotic possession sheds light on the truth and inspires true poetry, a poetry whose source is not "without" but "above." Dante and Plato both distinguish between the poet who is divinely inspired and the "imitative" artist, between the poet who writes what love dictates and the poet who simply writes.

Indeed, Dante calls our attention many times to the special divine gift of true poetry and to the unique character of the poet's activity. Unlike Plato's myths of the other world in the *Phaedrus, Phaedo, Gorgias,* and *Republic,* which are not reducible to a consistent whole and which he called useful lies,[10] Dante claims that his visions are not *falsi errori,* for consistent truths emerge from their symbolic content. The visions he saw rapt in an ecstasy are true, for his awakening is a turning from those things which are true within to those which are true without.[11] What Dante means might perhaps be clarified by a passage from *De monarchia* where Dante quotes St. Augustine as saying that in Scripture not everything told as having happened is to be taken as significant.[12] The insignificant is added for the sake of the significant. Thus, although the plowshare is the only part of the plow which actually cleaves the earth, the other parts of the plow are needed so that the plowshare can perform its function. This is a truly functional sense of myth and metaphor, the means of expressing what would otherwise be inexpressible. There are realities which can be understood only through symbol or narrative, not through abstract statement.

The most striking passage on the inspired nature of poetic truth, the affirmation that "poetry is the utterance of truth in terms of the imagination which cannot be otherwise known or told," [13] is in *Purgatorio* XVII, 13 ff., where Dante, in contradiction to St. Thomas and the Aristotelianism of the schools, says that visions and images enter the consciousness in the absence of sensation. Dante rejects the scholastic commonplace that *nihil est in intellectu quod non fuerit prius in sensu* and affirms that the divine light, directly or through the medium of the light of the heavenly bodies, may give the imagination its content.

O imagination, which so steals us at times from outward things that we pay no heed though a thousand trumpets sound about us, who moved thee if the senses offer thee nothing? A light moves thee which forms in the heavens, either of itself or by a will which directs it downwards.[14]

The divine aspect of poetic creation, the ability to imagine what the eyes have never seen or the ears heard, is presented later in the *Purgatorio* (XXIV, 48) as the dictation of love, the dictation of the Holy Spirit, a conception reserved in medieval theological and philosophical speculation for the inspired prophets of God who wrote the Sacred Scriptures. Bonagiunta says to Dante:

But tell me if I see here him that brought forth the new rhymes, beginning with *"Ladies that have intelligence of love."*
And I said to him: "I am one who, when love breathes in me, take note, and in that manner which he dictates within, go on to set it forth." [15]

Bonagiunta confesses that his pen as well as that of the Notary and Guittone did not follow close behind the "dictator." The difference between their poetry and that of Dante is thus the difference, in platonic terms, of poetry as imitation and poetry as inspiration. It is not only in this place that Dante calls our attention to a radical difference between the kinds of poets. It is one he frequently makes in *De vulgari eloquentia*. True poets need genius, constant practice, and the "habit" of the sciences. It is poets so equipped that Virgil calls beloved of God and children of the gods.[16]

Again, in the letter to Can Grande della Scala, Dante distinguishes between orators and poets precisely on the basis of inspiration. In the light of a tradition which tended to absorb poetry into the category of rhetoric this is especially significant:

For orators are wont to give a forecast of what they are about to say, in order to gain the attention of their hearers. Now poets not only do this, but in addition they make use of some sort of invocation afterwards. And this is fitting in their case, for they have need of invocation in a large measure, inasmuch as they petition the superior beings for something beyond the range of human powers, something almost in the nature of a divine gift.[17]

The poet thus surpasses the orator, rivals the philosopher, claims the same source of inspiration as the prophet, and accomplishes all this through being a lover. Love inspires him with the light of his truth and Love leads him through the light of his beauty.

For Plato, as we have seen, the poet and the lover take separate paths to the same goal as do the prophet and the theurge, for the four kinds of *mania* constitute, as it were, four converging lines to eternity. For Dante, on the other hand, the poet and the lover are one. Poetry is thus not the lowest form of knowledge but the rival of metaphysics. It is not a mere enjoyable lie but an avenue to ultimate reality equal to philosophy.

In both Dante and Plato the tensions between philosopher and poet were strong; both were men of speculative temper and of the greatest sensivity to beauty. The *Comedy* is, in one sense, the result of the resolution of those tensions between the lover, thinker, and poet as the *Phaedrus* and *Symposium* seem to be the resolution of similar tensions in Plato. Socrates "confesses" his betrayal of the god of love (*Phaedrus* 241D–243E), and, in effect, Dante confesses the same sin in his meeting with Beatrice in the *Purgatorio*. He had denied the God of love, ignorant of love and beauty as an avenue to the supreme reality.

In spite of all the similarities, there is one crucial difference between platonic Eros and Dante's "amore." The soul of the lover of beauty in both Dante and Plato ascends to immaterial beauty, but in Dante the beloved is not left behind on the bottom rung of the ladder, or at the first stage of the process. The beloved is transformed and elevated in her death —she achieves a greater, immaterial beauty—and precedes the lover up the ladder acquiring greater and greater degrees of beauty as she ascends. This difference, from one point of view, is a corollary of the importance Christianity gave to personality in its scheme of values and its plan of salvation. Its God is personal, and the death of one of the elect involves survival of personality as well as increase in value, in goodness and beauty. Dante turned to Beatrice after a period of error, doubt, and confusion because through her supernatural aid, her personal interest in him which survived death, he came to realize that he should have loved her more, not less, after she died.

The rivers Lethe and Eunoe in Dante do not obliterate the past, the complex of memories which constitute the essence of individuality; rather they purge guilt and reconstitute the wholeness and integrity which sin shattered. Memory, love, and the positive elements in personal relationships survive death. For Dante and Plato the ascent through love begins with the love of a concrete individual, but in Dante this is further intensified and concretized into the love for a person who remains a person throughout her ascent. Dante reconstituted the platonic doctrine of love and salvation through beauty, but only after taking into it certain elements of the Christian scheme of values.

In the final analysis, we find that Dante places the whole

erotic ascent in a charismatic framework. His experience is ultimately a result of grace, and grace is, so to speak, a personal relationship. It is a function of divine judgment and will, and those persons who are members of the community of saints play a part in its operation. Beatrice is sent to Dante's aid by St. Lucy, and the final transition, in the *Paradiso*, to the direct vision of the divine essence occurs when grace is asked through the prayers addressed in turn by Beatrice to St. Bernard, by St. Bernard to the Virgin, and by the Virgin to God. The grace to ascend to the beatific vision itself is, as grace, unearned and unmerited. It is dispensed to prayer, and Beatrice, a Florentine woman, is a link in the final chain of prayer at whose request the divine essence reveals itself.

Beatrice is thus a channel of grace. Dante's cosmology of love and light as beauty would have remained merely the framework of a possible salvation had there not been grace, and, in its ultimately incomprehensible way, it was bestowed through the instrumentality of the beauty of a person. All men, theoretically, can ascend the ladder of love, but all men in fact do not. This fact is the mystery of election. It was Beatrice, herself a surpassing *speculum*, who guided Dante through the universe of *specula*, through all the embodiments of divine beauty to the immaterial world of essence. It is, as he tells us, a natural journey,[18] the realization of a natural or cosmological possibility, not yet the achievement of beatitude which occurs only after Beatrice has done her work. Of course, even the journey with Beatrice is a gift of grace, but it is not of that fullness of grace which marks the transition from the natural to the supernatural order. In fact, the figure of Beatrice contains the whole moment of platonic Eros in Dante's system, in that she represents the flight to the Good. Platonic Eros had only this movement, from "here" up. Dante's "amore" has this movement, but it has an additional aspect, the love of God for man which makes his salvation possible and which makes the flight to God possible.

The existence of both the theoretical possibility of the erotic flight and Dante's realization of the possibility of that flight is ultimately to be seen as a process of election. We do not simply love the Beautiful, he loves us in turn. The "plain of truth" is a Person, or rather Three Persons. From one side, the ladder of love is pure Eros, from another it is a creation of pure agape, for the God of Love created the universe and ordered all things in it according to his providence.[19]

Virgil as well as Beatrice is a "natural" instrument of salvation, but they only remain possibilities unless they are actualized as instruments by God, and this actualization is charismatic. The ladder of love and beauty remains only a possibility unless we climb it. That it exists is a natural fact. That certain particular individuals climb it and others do not is a function of both grace and free will in the paradoxical relationship they have to each other in orthodox Christianity.

St. Bernard is not really so much an instrument of divine grace as one who explains its operation and actively requests it for Dante. It is with Bernard that we come to understand the gratuitous nature of the whole experience, and it is with Bernard that Dante leaves the natural completely behind and enters that world which is entirely of grace.

Let us now summarize the platonic conception of love and compare it with Dante's. What are the basic elements of Plato's thought on this question?

1. A ladder of love and beauty leads to an absolute reality.

2. Love is a dialectical progress through a hierarchy of various good and beautiful objects, a striving which cannot be satisfied except in the eternal possession of the Good and

Beautiful. The function of the various finite objects of desire is to "remind" us of a beauty once seen and presently forgotten, a beauty so great that we are impelled up the ladder of beautiful forms to possess it. Even if, as in later speculation, the notion of *anamnesis* is replaced with the idea of an implanted natural principle, a *nisus* to return to our Creator, the essential notion of love as a progress to the absolute is not modified.[20]

3. Love is also some kind of supernatural possession, an inspiration from above which leads to intuitions of truth, truth achieved through nonrational forms of apprehension such as are possessed by prophets and inspired poets. In this respect love appears as an ecstasy, the experience of direct and superrational contaction with the absolute. When it first manifests itself, it seems to be a form of madness, but this is only the beginning of the process. Eros, guided by judgment which distinguishes degrees of beauty, initiates a process which is nothing less than a journey to the source of Beauty, Good, Truth. Love as "possession" is thus the presupposition of love as a progress.

4. Man is endowed with a sense which enables him to grasp this beauty at its corporeal level and follow its ascent up to the highest. This sense is sight, and its organ is the eyes.

5. A beloved person is an individual who initiates Eros and "reminds" the lover of that perfect beauty once seen and now forgotten. This "recollection" is of perfect joy and satisfaction and awakens a desire to recapture perfect contentment and bliss and to have it everlastingly. The everlasting contemplation of Beauty, Good, and Truth implies death. There are desires which cannot be fulfilled in this mortal state, and the lover as well as the philosopher are both "learning to die." [21]

We now turn to Dante to see what we have found.

1. All sensible beauty, natural and human, is a reflection of divine immaterial beauty.

2. Things are so constituted that if their form or *species* completely dominates their matter, the bodily aspect of the thing translates or radiates its inner essence. This radiation is beauty, and it starts the erotic ascent which is at the same time the beginning of a process of knowing. Guided by judgment, desire passes from corporeal to incorporeal beauty and to the source of all beauty and truth.

3. Even as for Plato, the sense of sight is especially made for the apprehension of beauty, and there is a corresponding spiritual sense of sight which is involved in the apprehension of the immaterial forms of beauty. This higher sense really comes into play in the state of blessedness. In the presence of God there is no distinction between vision and thought, thinking and seeing. The condition of man is then such that he will directly see what in the mortal life he can only think.[22]

4. Man loves because he is not in his proper place. His home is heaven. When God created out of nothing man's unique and immortal soul, he implanted within it a natural desire to return to him who created it. Whether he is aware of it or not, all of man's desire for the innumerable finite embodiments or manifestations of beauty is a love of his Creator. In Dante this love is not only conceived as an implanted natural principle but also as the "recollection" of the joy and satisfaction which the soul experienced in its moment of contact with God when he made it. But Love, or the Holy Spirit, also inspires prophecy and true poetry.[23] Thus love is both a progress and a possession, both a *daemon* and a god.

5. The human being, the person, is one of these incarna-

tions of beauty and, in particular, the woman. As the form of a thing radiates beauty, so the soul or substantial form of a person radiates its beauty through the body.

It was Dante's achievement to place all these notions of love and beauty in an organic and dialectical relationship to each other and to introduce a particular beloved, a concretely conceived individual into the ladder of beauty to God. This is much more than the mere general recognition of the value and source of human beauty. It is a particular person with a name and a history who appears as a lure through the ladder of beauty. Both the platonic and Dantesque conception of salvation through love begins in a personal love, not in the abstract recognition of the fact that the human body is beautiful.

Thus what may be called the platonic vocabulary turns out to be a cosmology which permits the intelligible formulation of this experience. What may be called the experience of salvation through beauty is the actualization of what would otherwise have remained a mere theoretical possibility.

The chivalric element in Dante's conception of love, the ennobling power of the love for the *donna angelicata,* is not merely an attitude uncritically inherited from the past. The *donna* both of chivalric love and of Dante's Italian predecessors was never "thought out." The philosophical and theological speculation of Dante's time offered him a ladder of love and beauty to God, and the courtly poets offered him the image of an ennobling beloved without a ladder. Dante fused and synthesized these two traditions so that the world of chivalric love and the poets of the *dolce stil nuovo* became one rung of the *scala coeli* or *scala amoris.* No matter how fine or understandable, the love relationship which is final, which becomes an end in itself and is not transcended, can only become meaningless and lead to damnation. It should not be forgotten that Paolo and Francesca were reading about Lancelot on that fateful day. The positive elements of chivalric love are subsumed in a higher synthesis and reinterpreted in order to reconstitute the platonic doctrine of love.

At the heart of the experience of both platonic Eros and Dantesque "amore" is an almost prenatural sensitivity to beauty, a sense of what might be called its primacy. Where it exists, it is complete, overpowering in its fullness, not partial and fragmentary but whole and immediate. The raptures of Dante and the agonies of Plato's lover when they behold beauty are not hyperbole. The divine manifests itself primarily as beauty, and when we behold a beautiful object we are in some sense in the presence of divinity. Until the emergence of the modern scientific view of the world in the seventeenth century, the prevailing view was that the objects of consciousness were not merely things but signs and pointers as well. The universe had not yet become a mere aggregate of objects in a mechanical order. We might say that for both Plato and Dante the sign of signs, the quality in things which is the clearest clue as to their meaning and origin, is their beauty.

This sense of the primacy of beauty, of its divine origin and of its function as a lure leading men to the divine, also implied the corollary that love, art, and similar "irrational" activities had a higher status in the order of human activities than most of the rationalists of every age were willing to accord them. The creator and pursuer of beauty are both relating themselves in some direct and immediate way to the same ultimate reality which the philosopher seeks to comprehend.

The failure to understand what beauty might mean to a few supremely endowed men, and that there is a cosmology which can contain this meaning, has led to some of the problems—some of them pseudo-problems—of Dante scholarship. The allegorizers of Beatrice who dismiss the possibility that she could have been both a person and a personification, a "thing" and a "meaning," are victims of an inability to conceive an attitude and a universe which can give to human love such a staggering significance by relating it organically to absolute reality. As good a critic as John Addington Symonds, who refused steadfastly to allegorize Beatrice into nothingness, was unable to accept the platonic and Dantesque ideals of love as anything other than abnormal attitudes.[24]

Of course, not all critics and scholars who have concerned themselves with this problem have gone to extremes; yet, in spite of the sensitive and imaginative efforts of Moore, Williams, and Gilson we have not, it seems to me, been able to make the imaginative leap necessary to understand the experience from the center and not from the periphery.[25] For Beatrice, along with Virgil and St. Bernard, is one of Dante's guides through the whole universe; an otherwise unknown person is joined to two of the most famous men in the history of Western civilization, and she is described as a divinity, the "beloved of the First Lover" (*Par.* IV, 118). It is in attempting to understand Dante's extraordinary juxtaposition of the intensely personal with the universal that the comparison of Dante and Plato is most fruitful. For both these great lovers, a particular individual initiates the "journey of the mind to God." This individual is, from one point of view, ordinary, that is to say, no final reason can be assigned which will account for the fact that the lover finds the beginning of his salvation in the contemplation of his beloved. On the other hand, the beloved is unique in that the lover finds his beloved to be of surpassing and overwhelming beauty. Beatrice did not save the world, she helped to save Dante. Similarly, each lover must discover his own beloved and, in the image of Aristophanes' speech in the *Symposium,* find the other half he possessed before the gods split the original human race in two.

The unique role assigned to a person in initiating a desire which finds its fulfillment in eternity is, to my knowledge, peculiar to Dante and Plato before the revival of Plato in the Renaissance. Even that revival hardly seems to be more than a doctrinal one, not the expression of personal experience.

There are, of course, differences between the platonic and Dantesque ideals of love, and what some of these differences are has become more apparent. They serve, however, to highlight the startling parallels between the two. The two doctrines relate to each other like the two terms of a metaphor, with enough similarity to establish identity and enough difference to clarify the nature of that identity.

The most important general statement one might make about both these poets and philosophers of love is that they begin to consider love at the exact point where we leave off. Our modern pairs of lovers do not stand in relationship to anything outside themselves. But what is final for them is for Plato and Dante simply the beginning. What makes love intelligible is not its corporeal presuppositions but its *telos,* the goal of all its passion and striving. Love is not blind "attraction" in the sense in which modern physics uses the term, but conscious striving for eternity.

VI

Dante's Sun Symbolism
and the Visions of the Blessed

DANTE'S treatment of the doctrines of the light metaphysicians was both extraordinarily faithful to tradition and remarkably free in its handling of the materials he received. On the one hand, the properties of Dante's light are exactly what the metaphysicians of light said they should be; on the other, we find the freest sort of elaboration of what tradition merely hints at. Some of this elaboration is the work of pure imaginative power, a specification and concretizing of general principles. Much of the rest is the result of fusing light metaphysics with other structural principles derived from angelology, astrology, and such theological doctrines as the Mansions of Beatitude, the concept of various degrees of blessedness in paradise.

An example of Dante's fidelity to the truth of a concept can be found in his sun symbolism, and his bold freedom of invention is perhaps best seen in his rendering of the visions of souls in the *Paradiso*. Let us consider both of these themes in detail and turn first to his sun symbolism.

Light from the most ancient times has been symbolic of divinity. Man's natural revulsion before the darkness of the grave expressed itself as a striving toward the sun, toward the source of light and warmth, the very principle of life itself. The divinization of the sun and light finds expression in many of the religions of the East, especially Zoroastrianism, and even the Greek Olympians shone in a blazing splendor.[1] There is, of course, a great difference between the early mythological thinking which raises the sun or visible light to the status of a divinity and the biblical expression of God as light, which is rather an attempt to express a purely spiritual divinity through light symbolism. The appearance of God as a burning bush or as a pillar of fire is, however, some evidence of a residue of sun mythology. In Greek thought, the image of ultimate reality as light appears in the earliest period in Heraclitus' conception of the first principle as fire, a fire which is Zeus, the world order, and universal reason at the same time. This conception was developed by the Stoics and neoplatonists and culminated in the so-called light metaphysics of the thirteenth century.[2]

To indicate how Dante used the sun symbol with full awareness of the complex meanings it assumed in this tradition, we again return to Plato for our point of departure, to his famous analogy in the *Republic* between the Good and the sun (508B-C, 509B). Plato begins his discussion by maintaining that the artificer who made the senses was especially lavish with the sense of sight. All other senses have only two aspects, the active sense itself and the object of sense. Sight stands in need of a third factor, light, which is par excellence the property of the sun. Likewise there is a third factor needed between truth and the intellect. This is the Good, the sun of the realm of ideas. The sun of the sensible world stands in the same relation to vision and visible things as the Good of the intelligible world does to intelligence and intelligible things. Indeed, the sun is an offspring which the Good created in the visible world to fulfill a function of mediation analogous to its own. The Good is the cause of knowledge, of truth itself, and is of still higher worth than both of these. Just as light and vision are like the sun but not identical to it, so knowledge and truth are like the Good, different from and lower than it. There are thus two powers, the Good which reigns over the intelligible world and the sun which rules over the visible world. The one confers being on its world, the other is the principle of generation in its world.

The subsequent development of this doctrine of an intellectual light by Alexandrians, Stoics, Gnostics, and especially neoplatonists tended to emphasize a relationship of real filiation between intellectual and material light. The neoplatonists made light rather than the sun the highest principle of the visible world and affirmed that light, in the proper sense of the word, referred to an intellectual and immaterial light of which sensible light was a lowly derivative. It was in this form that the doctrine was known to the Middle Ages through the agency of Pseudo-Dionysius, the *Liber de causis*, and, most of all, the works of St. Augustine.[3]

St. Augustine adopted the famous platonic metaphor of the Good as the sun of the intelligible world, a metaphor widely used by both pagan neoplatonists and Christian fathers.[4] It is largely through his influence that the platonic interpretations of the sun symbol became widely diffused among medieval thinkers. We shall see that Dante was well aware of all the subtleties of this particular tradition of interpretation.

In Dante, the symbol of the sun appears in its primary function as the symbol of God. This is its simplest and most frequent meaning. Thus, Virgil says to Sordello: "Not for doing, but for not doing, I have lost the sight of the Sun above for which thou longest and which was known by me too late." [5] Similarly, in the *Paradiso*, after Charles Martel and Dante have finished speaking to one another, Charles turns to the Sun that fills his soul with the good that is sufficient for all things, himself a holy light contemplating the source of light. [6]

Appropriately enough, Dante makes an important distinction between the spiritual sun and the sensible sun when he enters the sphere of the sun. There Beatrice tells Dante to give thanks to the Sun of the angels, God, for having raised him to the visible sun. God, the immaterial sun, is not yet directly visible in the conditions of space and time, but Dante now sees his most complete analogue, the sun visible to the senses. [7] In the sphere of Jupiter, when the souls spell out *Diligite iustitiam qui iudicatis terram*, a cluster of souls, or "lights," settle on the letter *m* singing, Dante guesses, "of the good that draws them to itself." They gleam and soar as sparks struck from a burning log, shining and mounting above the letter to the degree that the Sun who kindles them ordains. [8]

As we draw closer to the final vision of the *Paradiso*, having left the sensible sun behind, the references are all to the intelligible sun, the sun who illuminates the spiritual host with the light of grace, good, and beauty. So Beatrice tells St. James that Dante's unsurpassed possession of the virtue of hope is written in the Sun that irradiates the host of heaven.[9] It is this sun who makes the perpetual spring of paradise, and odors of praise rise to it from the ranks of the blessed who make up the yellow of the eternal rose.[10]

God as the sun is the symbol of God as the highest and best. But the sun appears in another aspect in the platonic-Augustinian tradition. He is not only the source of all, the ultimate reality, but he also illuminates and mediates between the truth and the intellect. He is both Divinity itself and the source of the "light" which mediates the mind and the object of its knowledge. From this point of view the sun is a symbol of a being with powers of mediation. Thus the blessed saints in paradise are figured as burning suns who are simultaneously like "ladies not freed from the dance, but pausing in silence and listening until they have caught the new strain." [11] These dancing suns are the doctors of the Church who are mediators between the truth and the intellect. As saints they are intercessors and, in this sense, also mediators. The image of the sun as well as the placing of these doctors in the sphere of the sun is thus not arbitrary or merely convenient. In the light of the platonic tradition of sun symbolism there is no more appropriate place for those learned men who, more than any others, were a light between the truth and the intellect.

Analogously, both Pope and Emperor are suns, or rather this is what they used to be and ought to be once more: "Rome which made the good world, used to have two suns which made plain the one way and the other, that of the world and that of God." [12] In *De monarchia*, Dante had reluctantly accepted the traditional astronomical symbolism of the proponents of papal supremacy over the Emperor which conceived of the Pope as the sun and the Emperor as the moon. Dante argued, however, against the traditional interpretation of this symbolism which distinctly subordinated the Emperor to the Pope, the former merely reflecting palely the latter's light. With considerable ingenuity he maintains that, although the sun and moon were created on the fourth day, man was not created until the sixth. It is therefore inadmissible to argue that the two luminaries express the political supremacy of the Church over the Empire since they preexisted man and the need for both Church and Empire did not exist until man was created.

This argument is indeed strained, but it is interesting as an example of the way in which Dante believed that the symbolic value of things was "built into" them. The sun and the moon could not have the symbolic value the papal party wanted them to have because they were created before the realities they were intended to symbolize. They may stand for Church and Empire, but they cannot stand for the exact relationship between the two. In the *Paradiso* he discarded this whole line of argument and gave Pope and Emperor two equal expressions as suns and thus found a more consistent symbolism for what is essentially the thesis of the earlier work.[13]

St. Francis is the only saint explicitly singled out as a sun, an interesting image in view of the fact that Dante has been claimed as a Franciscan. Francis had been so symbolized before, but it may just be possible that Dante is giving St. Francis a special illuminating or mediatory function—personal or universal—by emphasizing the sun symbolism in his case.[14] However the matter stands with St. Francis, the major mediatory figures are clearly suns. Virgil, for example, is a sun who heals Dante's disturbed understanding, his intellectual vision.[15] More important still, Beatrice is a sun, the sun of his eyes, the sun who first warmed his breast with love.[16] These explicit references to Beatrice as a sun were adumbrated in

outlined

the *Purgatorio* when she was described as a light between the truth and the intellect, a "spiritual sun." This, as we recall, is identical to the platonic-Augustinian description of the Good or God as the sun of the intelligible world whose spiritual light provides the third factor necessary for knowing, the light which illumines truth and makes it accessible to consciousness.[17]

Thus for Dante, in agreement with platonic-Augustinian tradition, the sun is not only God, but the light which illuminates the path between the mind of the pilgrim and truth. This the intelligible sun does through the agency of lesser suns, the Pope and the Emperor, the saintly doctors of the Church, and, with special reference to Dante, through Virgil and Beatrice. Each lesser sun is a total but finite image of that infinite immaterial sun which is the goal of the pilgrim's journey, a *speculum* of the infinite.[18]

The symbol of the sun with its various meanings helps, in at least one instance, to give strength to a dramatic situation in the poem. In the *Purgatorio* Virgil invokes the sun whose rays are his guide:

"O sweet light by trust in which I enter on this new road," he said "do thou guide us wtih the guidance which is needful in this place. Thou givest warmth to the world, thou sheddest light upon it. Unless other reason urge the contrary thy beams must always be our guide." [19]

Virgil here addresses the physical sun, the sun of the sensible cosmos. Yet the full import of this invocation, its overtones of sadness, do not become fully clear until we recall a previous Virgilian reference to the sun:

"Through all the circles of the woeful kingdom" he answered him "I have come hither. Power from heaven moved me and by its help I come. Not for doing, but for not doing, I have lost the sight of the Sun above for which thou longest and which was known by me too late." [20]

Virgil knows that the sun to which he prays for guidance is really no more than the sensible analogue of the sun of the intelligible world from whose light he is forever cut off. Indeed even the light of purgatory, a sensible light, will be cut off from him, for he must return to limbo which is sad not with torments but with darkness.[21] So also, when Virgil questions Statius on how he happened to be saved, he uses the image of sun and candles as symbols, respectively, of divine or human mediatory illumination.[22] Thus Virgil, himself a sun for Dante, must spend eternity in darkness. The most of the sun he can see, and that only while guiding Dante, is the sensible mirror of the divine, the greatest and truest *speculum* of God,[23] but not God himself.

Not only is God the sun, the spiritual Helios who adorns and glorifies the blessed (*Par.* XIV, 131), but the various persons of the Trinity, since they are all one, are represented as suns. As all the stars derive their light from the physical sun, so the "living lights" of the blessed derive their light from the Holy Spirit. The image of God as the sun is thus transferred to the Third Person of the Trinity whose smile is externally translated as the shining of the blessed.[24] Analogously, in the *Paradiso* Christ appears as a sun who makes the blessed shine as the physical sun makes our heavens shine. Dante looks upon this "sun" and is blinded in an ecstasy.[25] In the previous canto (*Par.* XXII, 142) Dante had been able to bear the sight of the physical sun, something he had not at first been able to do without the aid of the strengthening and actualizing power of Beatrice's eyes (*Par.* I, 52 ff.). Now it is the intelligible sun whose sight is too strong for his vision.

Dante's eyes had been strengthened through the course of his
journey to such a degree that he was able to look upon the
brightest object in the physical universe without difficulty.
But in passing from the sensible to the intelligible universe,
from the sensible sun to the intelligible sun, he is again over-
whelmed, as always when passing from one level of the universe to the next higher one. The passage from physical sun
to intelligible sun is also an image for the beginning of the
transition from "speculation," the knowledge of God through
creatures, to the lower form of contemplation, the perception
of immaterial reality through images.

Beatrice had also called Christ a sun indirectly when she
told Dante to look upon the garden which flowers under
his rays.[26] Later in the same canto Dante picks up the image
of the sun shining on flowers and develops it, so that after
Christ ascends to the empyrean from his "appearance" or
manifestation in the starry sphere, he continues to illuminate
the souls even though, as sun, he is no longer directly visible:

As in the sun's rays streaming clear through a broken cloud my
eyes, sheltered by shade, once saw a field of flowers, so I saw
many hosts of splendours flashed upon from above by burning
rays, without seeing the source of the brightness.[27]

Although Dante is not able to see the "shining substance"
of Christ in Canto XXIII (l. 32) he is yet able to see the
Virgin, "the greatest of the fires" and the "living star" (90 ff.)
around whom the vision of the Church Triumphant centers
as the vision of the Church Militant centers around Beatrice.
Not only does Dante at last see the "shining substance" of
Christ in his final vision, but the Virgin, first a "living star,"
later becomes a sun that beautifies St. Bernard.[28]

It is important to note that the Virgin becomes a sun precisely at that point in Dante's narrative in which she is in-

voked as a mediator. It is at the behest of this "sun," the mother of God, that God, the intelligible sun, reveals himself to Dante.

Dante's conception of the blessed will now be examined to see how he enriches precisely where tradition left an undifferentiated luminosity.

As Dante journeys with Beatrice through the spheres, various groups of souls descend to meet them at the different planetary steps of the ladder to God. They are visually rendered as lights, at first with a shadow of the human semblance visible and later, after the brightness of the souls increases so that it hides their features, as pure lights. Dante employs a wealth of terms derived from light phenomena or luminous objects to visualize the spirits.

They are sometimes seen as flashing jewels, such as rubies, or a single light may seem a topaz (*Par.* XV, 85; XIX, 4–5; XX, 16). A soul may look like a candle (XI, 15) or, as that of Peter Damian, resemble a rapidly spinning luminous millstone (XXI, 80–81). St. John is a flaming circle (*infiammato giro*, XXV, 130), and he appears, along with the souls of St. Peter, St. James, and Adam, as one of four torches (XXVII, 10). Usually, however, the souls are simply lights of one sort or another without much visual differentiation or concrete suggestion in the epithet applied. The least specific soul name is "light," either *lume* (XIII, 29; XXIII, 110; XXIV, 153), which like Latin *lumen* refers to a form of radiated light, or *luce* (Latin *lux*), something luminous as a source of light, "Splendor" (XVII, 121; XXI, 32), the technical term for reflected light, is another frequent soul name. Less common is "effulgence" (*fulgor*, XVIII, 25), and "rays" seems to describe only the soul of Adam (*rai*, XXVI, 82).

Several other names are found for a soul light: "fire" (*fuoco*, IX, 77; XXII, 46; XXIV, 20; XXV, 37, 121; *incendio*,

XIX, 100; XXV, 80), "flame" (*fiamma*, XII, 2; XIV, 66; XXIII, 119), "flaming" (*fiammeggiare*, X, 103), "lamp" (*lucerna*, VIII, 19; XXI, 73; XXIII, 28; *lampa*, XVII, 5; XVIII, 25). No attempt has been made to give every reference for each word or to distinguish between its use in the singular or in the plural.

The number of terms is paralleled by the variety of formations and motions the souls display, en masse, in teams, and in figures, and by the way in which their increasing brightness and motion, individually or in patterns, signal their inner state—love, joy, depth of spiritual vision, or their desire to inform the eager pilgrim. By continually arranging and rearranging soul lights and changing light synonyms, Dante lends variety and concreteness to what might easily have been a rather monotonous and abstract landscape. In addition, our world is brought into the poem by what each particular vision of the souls suggests to the pilgrim in the way of an earthly counterpart. The *Paradiso* is rich with the imagery of dance and song, of flowers and meadows, and of all the familiar sights of our world—fish in a pool, the flight of birds, sparks leaping from a struck log, a stone sinking in a pond, stars in the sky.

This is one way in which Dante solved the artistic problem posed by the uniformity inherent in the very notion of eternal bliss. Heaven obviously lacks the excitement and variety of hell or purgatory, and Dante's task was to take a world of light, populated by lights, and differentiate it. Hence the number of similes in the final section is one-third more than is found in either of the other parts, for it is the imagery of the *Paradiso* which substitutes for the drama of the rest of the poem and makes it, in one sense, a prolonged lyrical pageant. A further structural principle was derived from the doctrine of the Mansions of Beatitude. The souls manifest themselves in their respective spheres, higher or lower as a sign of their various beatitudes, although they all really inhabit the one house of the empyrean. The cosmological hierarchy is thus a hierarchy of spiritual mansions, each level manifesting a different quality and greater intensity of light, more complexity in soul formations, and greater variety in the similitudes which define the soul lights.

We do not, however, see the souls as their similitudes. Rather, we are asked to transfer certain qualities and activities of our world to lights, to a reality which is far more abstract and which, in turn, is a manifestation of eternal reality in terms of space and time. The souls are seen simply as lights, until, in the empyrean, we finally see them as they really are. But these soul lights have varying qualities, and we experience them as differing among themselves, not simply because some of them speak to us and shine with a "various light" but because they suggest to the pilgrim numerous sights, sounds, and experiences of this world.

Thus the metaphors of the *Paradiso* are not always in the service of exact visualization, for the landscape has already been visualized, at least in general terms, by Dante's use of light imagery. Indeed, their function is often interpretive, and they define the nature of a reality already seen. An interesting example of this use of metaphor is found when the souls of the contemplatives descend the golden ladder to meet Dante. The poet here compares the movements of the luminous "splendors" to the movements of daws as, through instinct, they rise together at daybreak to warm their cold feathers and "some fly off without returning, some turn back to where they started, and some remain wheeling around, such that sparkling appeared to me as it came together and reached a certain step" (XXI, 37–42).[29]

The souls are not black and glossy like daws, however,

nor is their motion for the purpose of warming themselves even though they appear in the "cold" planet Saturn.[30] But, since their wills are subordinate to God's, their activity is analogous to the activity of those creatures who instinctively obey Nature, God's "child" (cf. *Inf.* XI, 97–105). Dante wants us to understand that the movements of the souls are of this kind, and what he wants us to see in the already visualized lights is the variety of their motions. In this respect only they look like daws.

Dante's rendering of the blessed is the most conspicuous of his manipulations of light for the first twenty-three cantos of the *Paradiso*, and an examination of each of his soul visions will reveal one of the important principles of structure of this section.

Dante first sees the blessed souls of paradise when he enters the moon. They there manifest themselves to him as luminous faces, seen clearly but as an image reflected from a piece of transparent glass or from a shallow pool. Dante further defines the quality of their appearance most strikingly by telling us that they stand out no more than would a pearl against the background of a white brow. The souls are here so pallid and so undifferentiated from their lunar background that Dante, taking them for reflections, turns round to find their realities but sees nothing (III, 10–21).

Beatrice is amused at Dante's error and tells him that what he took to be reflections are real and true substances, more real than the corporeal realities he sought in turning. For Dante, the signs of reality are still earthly—solidity and palpability—and he has not yet learned to trust in the actuality of the higher realities disclosed by spiritual and intellectual vision. Dante's error flows from the instinctive common-sense empiricism of everyman who finds it difficult to grasp that the real and the intelligible are one (25–33). Dante will not make this mistake again, for his increasing power of vision will permit him to grasp more of the substantial and intelligible light which constitutes the *Paradiso*.

In this sphere, Dante speaks with Piccarda Donati who, having finished her discourse, begins to sing and "singing vanished, like something heavy through deep water" (122–124).

In Dante's next encounter with the souls in the sphere of Mercury they appear as "splendors," individual lights shining as if reflecting light, and their movement suggests fish coming together in a calm, clear pond. The poet here first explicitly mentions the brightness of the souls, a shining which signals their happiness (V, 100–108). It is at this early stage of the heavenly journey that the souls—specifically that of Justinian—grow so bright that all human semblance is lost in the soul's own light (130–139). From now until the empyrean Dante will meet with lights rather than faces.

When Justinian is through with his history of the expansion of Rome, he begins to sing, spinning to his own song, and is joined by his companion spirits in a dance (VII, 1–8). They then all suddenly disappear in the distance like "swiftest sparks" (*velocissime faville*).

In the sphere of Venus the souls are visualized as lamps (*lucerne*) in a field of light, the planet itself, and suggest the appearance of a spark in a flame. They are further defined by a musical metaphor of a melody *flowing* above the note of the "canto fermo." The melody of lights counterpoints the long-held note of the luminous background, and the "lamps" circle round "faster and slower, in proportion, as I believe, to their eternal vision" (VIII, 16–27). Dante here translates the "figure-ground" configuration of spark and flame, or lamp and field of light, into its aural counterpart of melody and bass tone with stunning effect, using the non-visual metaphor precisely to define the quality of what is seen.

He again alludes to the activity of the blessed as a dance, for the divine lights come to him and Beatrice "leaving the dance [*giro*] previously begun among the high Seraphim" (26–27). The souls here move "in one circle, with one circling, with one thirst" (*d'un giro e d'un girare e d'una sete*, 35), constituting a ring or wheel (*rota*, IX, 65). This third image for the appearance of the souls, like the other two, suggests unity within multiplicity and motion within stillness, that fusion of life and art which is the only way we can grasp what a life transcending moral and intellectual effort might mean. Dante demands that we ask of his dancing lights what Yeats asked of his dancer: "O body swayed to music, O brightening glance. How can we know the dancer from the dance?"

Dante frequently imagines an important soul such as Piccarda or Justinian more concretely than its companions. Thus Rahab here appears as a radiance (*lumera*) which sparkles like a sunbeam in clear water (112–115).

After the ascent to the sphere of the sun, Dante calls our attention to the supreme brightness of the souls, so intense that they stand out against the sun itself, not by difference in color but by their even greater shining (X, 40–43). Then the flashing soul lights (*fulgor vivi e lucenti*) arrange themselves in a circle, a "crown" (*corona*, 65), with Beatrice and Dante as the center, singing even more sweetly than they shine.

So arranged, they suggest the halo that sometimes surrounds the moon (X, 64–69). They are also like gems or burning suns or like those stars which circle round the pole. After the crown of souls circles round the couple three times and stops, they appear like "ladies not freed from the dance" who, after dancing to their own song, pause until their leader should give them the signal to begin again. This time the actual motion of the team of souls is described as a dance (X, 76–81), an elaborate dance which goes on all through the canto, interpreted only by the speakers. The souls finally suggest plants in a garland (91–92) and a glorious wheel (*gloriosa rota*, 145).

In Canto XII, the circle of blessed in the heaven of the sun begins to turn like a holy millstone (*santa mola*, 3) and is immediately encircled by a second ring of spirits. These two rings together suggest a double rainbow as the first ring alone had suggested the lunar halo. The new circle of spirits is again a garland, but the figure is amplified, for both rings are now garlands or wreaths of eternal roses (10–21). Thus the poet completes the figure St. Thomas used when he told Dante that the pilgrim wanted to know what plants bloom in the garland of spirits (X, 91–92). The activity of the souls is again described as a dance (*tripudio*) but in the context of a "great festival of singing and flaming" (XII, 22–23). The term for dance here is not *ballo*, *danza*, or *giro* but *tripudio*, the word for the festival or religious dances of ancient Rome.

Dante describes the double ring with the same metaphorical material that he used to describe the single ring, but the lunar halo has become a double rainbow, the dance becomes a festival dance, and the garlands are specified as made up of roses.

He begins Canto XIII with a long and elaborate astronomical simile, singling out the fifteen stars of the first magnitude in medieval astronomy, the seven stars of the Great Bear (the Wain), and the two brightest stars of the Little Bear (the Horn) starting from the Pole Star, then asking us to rearrange the twenty-four stars in two concentric circles of twelve which revolve, as it were, following each other. We would then have a shadow of the real or true constellation which he saw. Unlike his reaction to the faces in the sphere of the moon, Dante now knows and has known ever since that experience what is truly real (1–21). The rings of souls circle in a "double dance" (*doppia danza*, 20) around him as a central point and as they turn sing of the Trinity and the Incarnation (25–27).

After the light of St. Thomas has explained to Dante the perfect creation of Adam and Christ and Solomon's gift of kingly understanding, Beatrice asks the spirits to tell them whether they will shine with their resurrected bodies and, if so, how their reconstituted eyes will be able to bear the intensity of each other's shining (XIV, 10–18). The souls show their new joy in this petition by renewing their circling and singing, "as those who dance in a round, at intervals raise their voices and quicken their movements with joy, impelled and drawn by greater happiness" ("Come, da più letizia pinti e tratti, / alla fiata quei che vanno a rota / levan la voce e rallegrano li atti," 19–24). Solomon, the "divinest light" of the first ring of spirits (34), explains the nature of their future resurrected bodies as he moves in his circle. Just after Solomon's speech, Dante sees a third ring of spirits beginning to form around the other two, as at evening new stars begin to appear in the sky, "stars" which we now see adding themselves to the constellation we were asked to make of the first twenty-four lights. This vision is interrupted by a sudden brightening, Beatrice becomes more luminous and beautiful, and Dante finds himself in the next higher sphere of Mars (XIV, 70–84).

The third ring of spirits which almost appears to Dante as he is whisked to the next higher sphere has been variously interpreted. In one view they are a sudden vision of angels. That of Benvenuto Da Imola, still the most plausible, is that they are a third ring of doctors of the Church. According to him, such great intellectual leaders of the Church have been so numerous that Dante could choose only some for actual representation and merely hint at a number of undefined others. He was unable to sound the depths of the teachings of so many. Benvenuto also assumed that the third ring was made up of thinkers who were less "right" than the other two, an assumption unjustified by the text. Still other early commentators more or less reverse this opinion and assume that Dante thus refers to thinkers who were too profound for him to comprehend, although this seems very unlikely.[31]

— In Mars, the souls appear as ruddy splendors, as greater and lesser lights such as make up the Galaxy, and they are gathered together in the form of a blood-red cross (XIV, 94–102). There is great activity in the cross of lights as the spirits move about in it flashing more or less according to their beatitude, and they look like numerous shining specks of dust in a sunbeam:

From horn to horn and between the summit and the base lights were moving that sparkled brightly as they met and passed; so we see here, direct and aslant, swift and slow, changing appearance, the particles of matter, long and short, move through the beam which sometimes streaks the shade that men devise for their protection with cunning and skill.[32]

Hitherto the teams of the blessed have grouped themselves as circles, rings, or garlands whenever they have assumed definite patterns. The circle is, of course, the "perfect" figure, and circular motion, literally or metaphorically, is the motion of the perfect fifth essence or of spirits. Indeed, at the very close of the journey Dante himself assumes a circular motion, the sign of the completion of his divinization. The cross, however, is a symbol with rich historical reference. It contains the universal drama of salvation and points to the central event of universal history. The warrior saints who made up the cross defended and carried it with them over the world, as the Emperors carried the eagle of Roman justice, the shape the souls assume in the next heaven of Jupiter.[33] In the heaven of Saturn we find a symbol of great philosophical significance when the souls are seen against the background of the golden ladder of contemplation.

This sequence of symbols gives us three of the most powerful and pervasive images of the medieval imagination. Unlike the individual soul lights, they are not symbol masks of a higher reality not yet visible as it is. They are rather the archetypal forms of earthly symbols of the highest significance, symbols which evoked so much of the thinking, feeling, and imagining of the men of the Middle Ages that an interesting part of the cultural history of that period might be written by organizing our material around them. If we add the mirror or *speculum* to the series, we might write even more of it, for medieval symbolism, exemplarism, and analogism, when it is not historical, rests on the notion that the created world reflects the immaterial divine essence in various ways and degrees and stands in a metaphorical relationship to it.[34]

From the first of these symbols, the cross of soul lights, a gem comes to greet Dante, the spirit of his ancestor Cacciaguida (XV, 19–24). After a long discussion of ancient Florence and his prophecy of Dante's fate, Cacciaguida begins to name the various spirits in the cross. As he does so, they shoot through it like lightning through a cloud, the spirit of Maccabaeus rotating as it moves (XVIII, 34–42).

In the sphere of Jupiter a team of spirits, golden lights, goes through a still more elaborate set of motions. As birds risen from a river bank, the souls form into various shapes and, letter by letter, spell out in Latin *Diligite iustitiam qui iudicatis terram*. They sing as they form each letter and are silent for a while when it is complete and before arranging themselves in the form of the next one (XVIII, 70–93). In the *m* of *terram* they rest and keep their order, appearing as gold points against the silver background of the planet; then other lights descend to the top of the letter, settle there, and then rise in different degrees in a shower of sparks like those struck from a burning log, to make those rising higher the head and neck of an eagle. The rest who did not so rise first form a lily on the *m* and then help to complete the rest of the eagle. This picture is the work of the Divine Artificer, and he impels each spark to move to its appointed place (XVIII, 94–111). The souls seem like brilliant rubies (XIX, 4–5) and suggest perpetual flowers to the pilgrim (22).

This pageant of lights is another allegory analogous to the procession of the Church Militant on the summit of purgatory and the pageant of lights in *Paradiso* XXIII symbolizing the Church Triumphant. The central spectacle of the latter is what might be called a transcendental representation of a historical event, the Annunciation with allusions to its momentous consequences. The archangel Gabriel in the shape of a luminous torch circles around the "star" which is the Virgin Mary immediately before all the souls follow Christ, the *psychopompos*, the sun of the new creation, up to the empyrean. This is a prospective vision of a triumph which is yet to be completed although it is eternally actual. Analogously, the eagle shows how the Guelph lily must dissolve and its component units be voluntarily absorbed as parts of the imperial eagle, a process which Dante believed to be under way although not yet completed. Yet in eternity it is somehow complete, and history moves inexorably toward its realization. That the association of all the smaller states in one universal

empire is to be such that it will preserve the individual character and liberty of its members is suggested when the individual souls constituting the eagle each breaks into its own
particular song of divine love (XX, 10–12).[35]

Although the eagle of justice is "the banner that made the
Romans revered to the world" (XIX, 101–102) and "the en-
sign of the world and its chiefs" (XX, 8), it tells of that
mysterious divine justice of which Roman justice is but a
part and temporal analogue, a truth symbolized by the eagle
wheeling to the notes of a mysterious and incomprehensible
song (XIX, 97–99). The myriad souls who constitute it
usually speak and sing and wheel as one, however, manifesting
that perfect harmony of many wills in one perfect willing of
a perfect good which is what all earthly justice aspires to but
cannot achieve. Yet, whatever we have of justice here below
is nothing but the effect of the influence of that heavenly
sphere and its planet (XVIII, 115–117).

Here is the apotheosis of the imperial ideal which so
haunted the minds of the men of the Middle Ages, the transcendental eagle whose earthly flight recounted by Justinian
(VI) gave the world all it ever knew of justice. Divine and
human justice are not really in an unalterable antithesis to one
another, as they are for St. Augustine, but the former completes the latter even though it transcends it. Indeed, Justinian
was divinely inspired to perfect that great body of law which
is, for Dante, the temporal instrument of divine justice (VI,
10–12).

As individual souls were singled out in the cross, so the just
rulers are singled out in the eye of the eagle (XX, 31–72).
When Dante is astonished at the presence of the pagan Ripheus
in paradise, the eagle team responds to his wonderment by
flashing (XX, 84), and the just rulers in the eye of the eagle
shine more brightly than before (XX, 85). As everywhere in

the *Paradiso,* brightness is the sign of the spiritual state of every kind of intellect—divine, angelic as in the case of the movers of the planets or of the beatified human soul. Everywhere Dante is welcomed by brightness, and the joy of shared love and knowledge is signaled by increase of light. Dante's last memory of the image of the eagle is of seeing the two lights of Trajan and Ripheus move their little flames as the eagle tells of the miraculous grace which permitted their salvation (XX, 145–148). Thus, our attention is gradually drawn from the innumerable lights that make up the eagle to the lights in its eye and then to two of the many.

In the sphere of Saturn, Dante sees a golden ladder which stretches upward into infinity with many soul lights, "splendors" descending the steps, in such numbers that they equal the number of stars: like daws, the sparkling mass of souls scatter, fly back and forth, and wheel about (XXI, 25–42).

The light that first comes to greet Dante here is that of Peter Damian, who spins around his own center like a rapid millstone (XXI, 80–81). The wheeling of the soul lights in this sphere makes them more luminous and beautiful as they descend the ladder (136–138). A smaller number of the myriad lights separates itself out and manifests itself to Dante as a "hundred little spheres of light which beautified each other with their mutual rays" (XXII, 23–24).

The largest and most lustrous of these "pearls" is St. Benedict (28–29), who explains that the ladder extends to the empyrean where Dante will see all the blessed not as lights but as they will be after the resurrection (58–69). The ladder is, of course, Jacob's ladder, the ladder of contemplation which no one on earth climbs any longer (70–78). But it suggests, too, all the many ladders in the medieval universe— the *scala Dei,* the *scala amoris,* the ladders of beauty, goodness, and being. It is the archetype of all the hierarchies, philosophical, theological, and social, which medieval thinkers used to organize and interpret experience.

The next great vision of souls, this time of all the souls in heaven, "all the fruit gathered by the revolutions of these spheres" (XXIII, 21–22), occurs in the starry heaven. Here they are seen as thousands of lamps (*lucerne*) kindled by the Sun which is Christ (XXXIII, 28–33). The souls no longer form symbolic patterns, nor, as in the case of the ladder, are they metaphorically related to a symbolic structure. We have come very close to the limits of the physical universe, to God, and it is significant that Dante should call our attention to the fact that the soul lights are illuminated with divine light and are not, as we may have assumed hitherto, in one way or another the source of their own brightness. In a beautiful simile he calls our attention for a second time in this canto to their derived light:

As in the sun's rays streaming clear through a broken cloud my eyes, sheltered by shade, once saw a field of flowers, so I saw many hosts of splendors flashed upon from above by burning rays, without seeing the source of the brightness.[36]

Dante then sees the Virgin Mary, "the greatest fire" (*lo maggior foco*, 90), "a living star" (*viva stella*, 92), and a "beautiful sapphire" (*bel zaffiro*, 101). As he watches her, the archangel Gabriel descends like a torch and circles about the Virgin assuming the likeness of a crown (94–96). At his request, the Virgin ascends to the empyrean so distant from where Dante is that his eyes are not able to follow the "crowned flame [*coronata fiamma*] that rose after her seed" (119–120). Each of the soul lights (*candori*) of this sphere reaches upward with its flame after Mary as she ascends, apparently like comets (124–125). This time the souls dramatically change their shapes instead of operating in teams, varying their shining or motions or changing color to look like various precious stones.

In this sphere, Dante will be examined on the three theological virtues, and, before St. Peter comes to test him on faith, the souls each spin on their own axes at various speeds like spheres on fixed poles, flaming brightly like comets (XXIV, 11–12). St. Peter, the brightest and most dynamic of the lights in this mass (cf. XXVII, 11–12), emerges to conduct the poet's examination. Analogously, just before St. John is to examine Dante on love, he shines out with a great brightness and joins the soul lights of St. Peter and St. James in their singing and their dance like a happy maiden who dances to do honor to the bride. The bride is implicitly Beatrice, for she looks upon the dancing apostles "just like a silent and motionless bride" (XXV, 100–110).

After Dante's three examinations, all the "triumphal vapors" (*vapor triunfanti*) that had manifested themselves to him throughout his journey return to the empyrean like snowflakes falling upward. The "unnatural motion" here reminds us of its demonic counterpart in the rain of fire that, contrary to the natural motion of this element, falls on the sodomites in the *Inferno*. We are thus again reminded that the unnaturality of heaven is of a supernatural kind and not, so to speak, "subnatural," a perversion of nature.

In the crystalline sphere, we no longer see souls but angels. These pure intelligences are also described as lights (*lume*, XXVII, 59), and they reflect divine light like mirrors (XIII, 94), but now we see all the orders of angels in a symbolic manifestation, as concentric circles of light around a point of light of infinite intensity. The circles closer to the point, God (cf. XVII, 17), move faster and shine brighter to the extent that they participate in the truth of the "pure spark" (*favilla pura*, XXVIII, 38). As always in the *Paradiso*, intensity of light and rapidity of motion signal depth of knowledge and love (16–39).

When Dante passes the limits of space and time and begins to acquire a new sight which will fit him to gaze on eternal realities as they are, he first sees the empyrean as a river of light. Its banks are covered with flowers—the blessed of both Testaments—and "living sparks," angels, leap out of the torrent of light to settle on the flowers "like rubies set in gold" and then plunge back into the river of divine grace (XXX, 61–69). This vision, as Beatrice tells him, is an adumbration of its reality, not yet the reality itself (76–81). After Dante "drinks" of the river of light with his eyes, as he must to gain the requisite power of vision, he sees "both the courts of heaven," angels and blessed, clearly (94–96).

Dante now sees the blessed in their human shapes, with their bodies as they will have them after the resurrection, seated in tiers in the petals of the rose (113–120). The angels appear with faces of living flame, wings of gold and the rest white, ascending and descending from the rose of the blessed to God, importing peace and love (XXXI, 1–18). The sparks which flitted in and out of the river of light are now clearly seen as pictorial angels, the flowers on the banks of the river are now human shapes, and the torrent of light is now the "threefold light [*trina luce*] which, as a single star" shines on them all (28–29).

What is most remarkable about this final vision is the sudden transition to an intensely concrete and literal vision of the blessed and the angels after the gradually growing abstractness of the heavenly landscape. We began by seeing human features dimly through the light which is the substance of the blessed. This light increases in intensity, like the light of the spheres and of Beatrice, as we ascend to the empyrean. In the sphere of Mercury the substantial light of the souls grows so bright that it hides any human semblance. Thereafter we see nothing but lights, although they speak, sing, "dance," arrange themselves in patterns, and vary their brightness. Nevertheless, we experience them as qualitatively different not only because of who they are and what they say or because of the visual differences between them—they are relatively slight—but because of the earthly experiences to which they are metaphorically related.

Thus, although Dante's strictly poetic universe is always rich, his visual and conceptual universe grows more and more abstract—truths of progressively higher and more inclusive orders are made known, and less and less of the earth appears in the actual landscape. We might therefore expect Dante's universe to dissolve into pure light after he passes from time to eternity, and, if Dante had been a pagan neoplatonist, it would have done so.

In the case of the final vision of God, it appears to do just that, but there is a dramatic introduction of the concrete when Dante detects the human figure in the three concentric circles, the triple rainbow of light, which is the Trinity (XXXIII, 115–132). God is seen as light but is also seen as the Trinity and the Incarnation; the souls are seen as lights but they are finally seen in the concreteness they will possess with their resurrected bodies; the angels are seen as concentric circles of light, but they are finally seen as if they might have come from the brush of Giotto.

It is precisely in a realm theoretically and philosophically most unlike our universe that the colors and shapes of the human are dramatically introduced. Philosophy alone would have led Dante only to the One, a bland unity of pure light,[37] but Dante's faith led him to a world in which individuality is eternalized and the divine is somehow differentiated within itself as human.

⋇

Notes

I: Dante and the Phaedrus Tradition of Poetic Inspiration

1. On the sources and channels of transmission of medieval platonism see Raymond Klibansky, *The Continuity of the Platonic Tradition during the Middle Ages* (London, 1950). Various volumes of the
Corpus Platonicum Medii Aevi have appeared, and others continue to
be published from time to time. Although the *Phaedrus* and *Symposium* were unknown in the West, the elements of the doctrines contained in these works were widely diffused. The ladder of love and
beauty to God were cornerstones of much medieval theological
speculation. To reconstitute the Phaedrus doctrine, it was simply
required to synthesize love of beauty in a person with the amorous
ascent to God. Cf. also Bruno Nardi, *Dante e la cultura medievale* (2d
ed.; Bari, 1949), Preface and ch. i.

2. G. B. Burch, *The Steps of Humility by Bernard, Abbot of Clairvaux* (Cambridge, 1950), 77–81. Unless otherwise indicated the lengthier translations from the *Divine Comedy* are from *The Divine Comedy*, with translation and commentary by John D. Sinclair (rev. ed., 3 v.; London, 1948). The text of Dante's *Comedy* is that of the *Società Dantesca Italiana* (*Le opere di Dante Alighieri* [Firenze, 1921]). The *Liber de intelligentiis* is edited by Clemens Baeumker in *Witelo, ein Philosoph und Naturforscher des XIII Jahrhunderts* (in *Beiträge zur Geschichte der Philosophie des Mittelalters*, Band III, Heft 2; Münster, 1908). This work contains a long study of the light-metaphysics tradition. For medieval speculation on beauty see Edgar De Bruyne, *Etudes d'esthétique médiévale* (3 v.; Bruges, 1946). On the "aesthetic" of light see especially ch. i and ii in vol. 3. References to St. Thomas are to the Leonine edition of the *Summa theologiae* (*Opera omnia* [Romae, 1882–1930], vols. 4–12) and to the Vivès edition of other works (*Opera omnia*, ed. E. Fretté and P. Maré [34 v.; Paris, 1871–1880]); to St. Bonaventura, in the Quaracchi edition (*Opera omnia*, ed. P. P. Collegii S. Bonaventurae [10 v.; Quaracchi, 1882–1902]); and to St. Augustine and Rupertus Tuitens, in Migne's *Patrologia Latina*. The *Confessions* are in vol. 32, *The City of God* in 41, *On the Trinity* in 42, *Enarrations on the Psalms* in 37, and Rupertus Tuitens' works in 156. *P.L.* and *P.G.* refer to the Migne Latin and Greek series respectively.

3. On the powers—truly natural—conferred by the recovery of Eden, Dante says:

> Molto è licito là, che qui non lece
> alle nostre virtù, mercè del loco
> fatto per proprio dell'umana spece (*Par.* I, 55).

"Much is granted there that is not granted here to our powers, by virtue of the place made for possession by the race of men."

Also in Canto I, Beatrice explains the divine order of things and describes how all things are impelled by an innate natural principle of motion to seek their proper place in the universe. Man's place is with God and, freed from the incumbrances of sin, reconstituted as truly natural, he just as naturally ascends to God. *Par.* I, 136:

> Non dei più ammirar, se bene stimo
> lo tuo salir, se non come d'un rivo
> se d'alto monte scende giuso ad imo.
> Maraviglia sarebbe in te, se, privo

d'impedimento, giù ti fossi assiso,
com'a terra quiete in foco vivo.

"If I am right, thou shouldst no more wonder at thy ascent than at a stream falling from a mountain height to the foot; it would be a wonder in thee if, freed from hindrance, thou hadst remained below, as on earth would be stillness in living flame."

In this instance, the journey is described in terms of a natural journey through the sensible world, the physical cosmos. In *Par.* IV, there is a natural journey through the intelligible world. The intellect can never rest but in God, and this striving is motivated by doubt. *Par.* IV, 124:

Io veggio ben che già mai non si sazia
nostro intelletto, se 'l ver non lo illustra
di fuor dal qual nessun vero si spazia.

Posasi in esso come fera in lustra,
tosto che giunto l'ha; e giugner pòllo:
se non, ciascun disio sarebbe frustra.

Nasce per quello, a guisa di rampollo
a piè del vero il dubbio; ed è natura
ch'al sommo pinge noi di collo in collo.

"I see well that our intellect is never satisfied unless the truth enlighten it beyond which no truth can range. In that it rests as soon as it gains it, like a beast in the lair; and it can gain it, else every desire were in vain. Doubt, therefore, like a shoot, springs from the root of truth, and it is nature that urges us to the summit from height to height."

4. *Par.* XXX, 56.

5. *Par.* XXX, 40.

6. *Par.* VII, 58.

7. *Pur.* XXIV, 52.

8. Cf. *Conf.* I, 13; *De civ. Dei* XVIII, 13; II, 14; VII, 13.

9. *In De anima* I, 12; *In Metaphysicorum libros* I, 3; XII, 6.

10. *Summa theologiae* 1, q. 1 a. 9 ad 1.

11. See Régis Jolivet, *Dieu Soleil des esprits* (Paris, 1933), for the Augustinian doctrines of light.

12. St. Thomas Aquinas, II *Sent.* d. 13 q. 1 a. 2. Cf. (Utrum lux proprie inveniatur in spiritualibus) Dicendum quod in hoc videtur esse quaedam diversitas inter sanctos. Augustinus enim videtur velle, quod lux in spiritualibus verius inveniatur quam in corporibus, sed

Ambrosius et Dionysius [i.e., Johannes Damascenus] videntur velle, quod in spiritualibus non nisi metaforice inveniatur.

St. Thomas gives St. Augustine a little credit on this, however: "Et quantum ad hoc verum est dictum Augustini, quod lux verius est in spiritualibus quam in corporalibus, non secundum propriam rationem lucis, sed secundum rationem manifestationis." Cf. Eph. 5:13 for the meaning of the term *manifestatio*.

In rejecting St. Augustine's notions on light (II *Sent.* d. 13 q. 1 a. 3) St. Thomas simply attributes Augustine's opinion to the philosophy which he learned in his time. His authority in this matter is therefore not compelling: "Nihilo minus Augustinus non intendit hoc afferre quasi fidei conveniens, sed sicut utens hic quae philosophiam addiscens audierat."

On scriptural use of metaphor see St. Thomas, I *Sent.* prol. a. 5, and Nancy Lenkeith, *Dante and the Legend of Rome* (London, 1952), 33 ff., for other references.

13. In *Quodl.* VI q. 11 a. 19 St. Thomas rejects the authority of the *De intelligentiis* on the notion of light as the actualizing principle.

14. *De intelligentiis* c. VI: Prima substantiarum est lux. Ex quo sequitur, naturam lucis participare alia. Hoc manifestari potest per auctoritatem Augustini in II super Genes. ad litteram docentis, quod Deus non dicitur lux, sicut dicitur agnus. Dicitur agnus translative et non proprie, lux autem dicitur proprie et non translative.

The author erroneously cites Book II of St. Augustine's work instead of Book IV.

15. *De intelligentiis* c. VII: Omnis substantia influens in aliam est lux in essentia vel naturam lucis habens. He continues: Si enim a substantia prima [i.e., God] est influentia in omnibus aliis, omnis autem substantia influens in aliam est lux in essentia vel naturam lucis habens.

16. *De intelligentiis* c. VI: Quod autem in istis sensibilibus apparentibus maxime est nobile, hoc est lux.

Cf. also (c. VIII) the following propositions: Unumquodque quantum habet de luce, tantum retinet esse divini.

Unaquaeque substantia habens magis de luce quam alia dicitur nobilior ipsa.

Perfectio omnium eorum quae sunt in ordine universi est lux.

. . . participatio lucis est participatio esse divini.

Notes to I: Phaedrus Tradition

On *nobilitas* as a synonym of light and beauty see De Bruyne, *op. cit.*, 3: 21 ff.

17. *De intelligentiis* c. IX: Lux in omnia viventi est principium motus et vitae calore disponente.

Ibid., c. X: Proprium et primum principium cognitionis est lux. Si autem exordium cognitionis inspexerrimus, dicemus: lux est ipsa virtus cognoscitiva.

18. *De intelligentiis* c. VIII: He sums up the hierarchy of light as follows: "Unaquaeque enim substantia in ordine universi magis habens de luce quam alia dicitur nobilior ipsa; nobilitas vero in omnibus attenditur secundum appropinquationem maiorem et participationem esse divini." There follows an example of the hierarchy of light: "Aqua enim magis habet de luce quam terra et in hoc dicitur nobilior ipsa. Aer vero quam aqua, et ignis quam aer, et corpus quintum magis quam omnia alia, et propter hoc nobilissimum et primum dicitur inter ipsa."

The light metaphysicians generally employed the language and imagery of emanationism although they did not derive the monistic and pantheistic consequences conclusive of this theory. They accepted the notion of creation and tried to reconcile it with the neoplatonic picture of the One as a point of light from which the universe derives by a kind of outpouring radiation of light (*profluxus* or *defluxus*). Like the neoplatonists, they looked upon physical light as something that thinned and purified itself as it converged to the point—the One or God—to which thought moved as it lost more and more of its abstractness and gained more and more vividness. Thought or mind finally merged with the point *in* achieving and *upon* achieving a "new sight" capable of seeing a light which is supersensuous and supernatural. The hierarchically ascending efficaciousness of light is a particular phase of a general doctrine which was widely diffused in the thirteenth century through the neoplatonic tract *De causis*, a work frequently cited by Dante. The doctrine in question states that a form discerned in matter is but a defective manifestation of the same power as it exists apart from matter (esp. Props. 1, 2, and 4; in *Die pseudoaristotelische Schrift ueber das reine Gute*, ed. Otto Bardenhewer [Freiburg im Breisgau, 1882], 163–168).

19. St. Bonaventura, II *Sent.* d. 13 a. 2 q. 2 pag. 312 a. Cf. De Bruyne, *op. cit.*, 3: 21 ff. St. Bonaventura also says of light, "Light is that by

which the body is united to the soul and that by which the soul rules the body" (II *Sent.* d. 15 a. 1 q. 3 f. 2 ad opp. pag. 379 b), and again (in IV *Sent.* d. 49 p. 2 sec. 1 a. 3 q. 1 pag. 1016 a), "The disposition which a body must have in order to live is fulness of light and *claritas.*"

20. *De intelligentiis* prop. XII: Lux inter omnia apprehensioni est maxime delectabile, quod est quia maxima delectatio est in conjunctione convenientis cum convenienti. Ergo si subjectum cognitionis [i.e., the soul] vel virtus cognoscitiva est lux, ex unione lucis exterioris cum ipsa (luce interiori) est delectatio maxima.

21. Rupertus Tuitens, *In Genes.* I c. 11; *P.L.*, 167: cols. 207 sq. Nec vero pro similitudine, sed pro re vera lucem dicimus appellatam (sc. angelicam naturam), id est non ideo quod similitudinem visibilis lucis habet. Nam ista potius visibilis lux, haec astra visibilia secundum similitudinem lucis illius sunt facta, ut cognoscat spiritualis homo, sic sanctos angelos in eodem felicitate differentis esse honoris et gloriae, sicut "stella differt a stella in claritate" (I Cor. 15, 41), sic eos in comparatione solis aeterni, scilicet creaturis sui, hemisphaerio nequeunt suum lumen ostendere.

Thus compared to sensible light, the angels are true light; compared to God (the "sun"), they are not. He is the true light.

22. E.g., *Pur.* XIV, 148.

23. *Par.* XXX, 108.

24. *Par.* II, 114.

25. *Par.* XXVIII, 41. Aristotle's *Metaphysics*, Bk. XII, c. 7, 1072 b.

26. II *Sent.* d. 13 a. 2 q. 2 ad 5 pag. 321 b.

27. *Par.* XXXIII, 91. My translation.

> La forma universal di questo nodo
> credo ch'i'vidi, perchè più di largo
> dicendo questo, mi sento ch'i'godo.

Sinclair has: "I think I saw the universal form of this complex, because in telling of it I feel my joy expand."

28. E.g., *Par.* II, 143.

29. *Par.* V, 96.

30. *Par.* XXI, 83:

> Luce divina sopra me s'appunta,
> penetrando per questa in ch'io m'inventro
> la cui virtù, col mio veder congiunta,
> mi leva sopra me tanto, ch'i'veggio

la somma essenza della quale è munta.
Quinci vien l'allegrezza ond'io fiammeggio;
perch'alla vista mia quant'ella è chiara
la chiarità della fiamma pareggio.

31. *Par.* XIV, 37:

Quanto fia lunga la festa
di paradiso, tanto il nostro amore
si raggerà, dintorno cotal vesta.
La sua chiarezza seguita l'ardore;
l'ardor la visione, e quella è tanta,
quant'ha di grazia sovra suo valore.
Come la carne gloriosa e santa
fia rivestita, la nostra persona
più grata fia per esser tutta quanta;
per che s'accrescerà ciò che ne dona
di gratuito lume il sommo bene,
lume ch'a lui veder ne condiziona;
onde la vision crescer convene,
crescer l'ardor che di quella s'accende,
crescer lo raggio che da esso vene.

32. St. Augustine develops this conception of the function of beauty from a more profound and extensive point of view. Beings not only know (*noscunt*) God but also reflect his truth, they make him to be known (*innotescunt*). Man does both of these things, but the lower creatures can do only the latter. In so doing, however, they aid rational man in his understanding of God. This unconscious manifestation of divine power in inanimate beings, this *innotescere,* is nothing else than what we call beauty. Language, the Augustinians said with dubious semantics, gives evidence of this truth. A beautiful thing (*pulchrum*) is called *speciosa* or *formosa* because its inner form (*forma*) is fully stamped in matter. Beauty is a function of being, it is the "exterior" translation of the "inner" essence. See *De civ. Dei* XI, 27; XVII, 16; *De Trin.* XV, c. 12, no. 21; *Enarr. in Psal.* 144 n. 13; Chapter III below.

33. The *Phaedrus* was the keystone of the neoplatonic system, and the neoplatonists systemized its central doctrines in their theory of salvation through love *extasis*. They gave us a rationale for finding God progressively as a result of speculative activity. The *extasis*, however, comes only to those who are prepared to receive it, and after a long

preparation. It is actually a theory of mysticism as a result of learning. The body and reason are points of departure for ecstatic visions, and the goal of the effort was the achievement of happiness or salvation (*soteria*) rather than knowledge as such. The aim of this kind of mysticism was, therefore, "practical" rather than contemplative although learning and contemplation were indispensable.

The system is really the description of the attempt to return to God through things made, the return being possible through the love that is in us, the love which is a divine gift and which in man is, in a sense, "man-made," i.e., man has free will. In the lower orders this love is not inherent as it is in man, it does not depend on a free appetitive faculty, but is divinely ordained and is nothing less than nature, the orderly purposefulness of the universe.

Plato's ladder of love is the endeavor to connect the world of ideas with our world. The first step is eros, eros as the unification of bodies. This is accompanied by a dissatisfaction so great that the dialectic process begins, the search for the one through the many, for unity through multiplicity. Further unification—the explanation of multiplicity—was possible through understanding. Thus the dialectic process which gives the one through the many is prosecuted through love, by adhering to the ladder of beauty. For the world of perception, understood in the light of the world of ideas, offers us a ladder to ideas themselves. Love brings us up this ladder which has more beauty and goodness on each rung. Indeed we only see the world of perception because we in some way have or partake of the world of ideas. Ideas do not need particulars to exist, but particulars need them. They are real above and beyond man, and the process of rising to them begins with sense as its *occasion*. The great problem for the neoplatonists whether pagan or Christian—as for speculation—was the relation between the changing world of sense and the demand of thought for stablity. In formulating a system of thought which would "save appearances" they decided to start from *genesis*, rise to *ousia* or essence, and unify the system through the ladder of love and beauty. Love thus appears as the *virtus unitiva*.

The neoplatonists of course desired not merely to reduce all to thought or "Ideas" but to go even beyond, since they found a duality in thought itself. Love as the *virtus unitiva* was the means for transcending even this duality, and it leads us to a beatitude which is beyond sense and thought, beyond matter and mind, and which is achieved in *extasis*. This is the culmination of a process which is both amorous and intellectual and which, beginning with the world of sense, proceeds through and beyond the intelligible world to absolute unity. The absolute is beyond reason, and love is the only power which enables us to reach it. See Amandus Bielmeier, *Die neuplatonische Phaidrosinterpretation* in *Rhetorische Studien,* Heft 16 (Paderborn, 1930).

34. *Summa theologiae* 1–2, q. 27 a. 1 ad 3.

35. *Vita nuova* XIV, 34–43, in *Le opere di Dante Alighieri,* ed. Edward Moore and Paget Toynbee (4th ed.; Oxford, 1924). References to minor works of Dante are to this edition unless otherwise indicated.

36. *Conv.* III, viii, 3–4; cf. *Conv.* III, ii, 14; III, vi, 11–12; III, vii, 8 ff. All references are to *Il Convivio,* ed. G. Busnelli and G. Vandelli (2d ed., 2 v.; Firenze, 1953–1954).

37. *Conv.* III, viii, 10–11.

38. *Vita nuova* XIX, 134–140: Ed acciocchè quinci si levi ogni vizioso pensiero, ricordisi chi ci legge, che di sopra è scritto che il saluto di questa donna, lo quale era delle operazioni della bocca sua, fu fine de'miei desiderii, mentre che io lo potei ricevere.

We might recall here the Aristotelian dictum that to smile is the property (*proprium*) of a rational being. It is something, not his essence, which every man possesses but which can be found nowhere else. The emphasis on the smile as being even more beautiful than the eyes is thus rooted in a philosophical distinction. Cf. *De part. anim.* III, 10, 673 a.

39. *Pur.* XXX, 121:

> Alcun tempo il sostenni col mio volto;
> mostrando li occhi giovanetti a lui,
> meco il menava in dritta parte volto.
> Sì tosto come in su la soglia fui
> di mia seconda etade e mutai vita,
> questi si tolse a me, e diessi altrui.
> Quando di carne a spirto era salita
> e bellezza e virtù cresciuta m'era,
> fu'io a lui men cara e men gradita;
> e volse i passi suoi per via non vera,

imagini di ben seguendo false,
che nulla promission rendendo intera.
Nè l'impetrare ispirazion mi valse,
con le quali ed in sogno e altrimenti
lo rivocai; sì poco a lui ne calse!
Tanto giù cadde, che tutti argomenti
alla salute sua eran già corti,
fuor che mostrarli le perdute genti.

40. *Pur.* XXXI, 46:

Pon giù il seme del piangere ed ascolta:
sì udirai come in contraria parte
mover dovìeti mia carne sepolta.
Mai non t'appresentò natura o arte
piacer, quanto le belle membra in ch'io
rinchiusa fui, e sono in terra sparte;
e se 'l sommo piacer sì ti fallìo
per la mia morte, qual cosa mortale
dovea poi trarre te nel suo disio?
Ben ti dovevi, per lo primo strale
delle cose fallaci, levar suso
di retro a me che non era più tale.
Non ti dovea gravar le penne in giuso,
ad aspettar più colpi, o pargoletta
o altra vanità con sì breve uso.
Novo augelletto due o tre aspetta;
ma dinanzi dalli occhi si pennuti
rete si spiega indarno o si saetta.

41. *Par.* XXVII, 88:

La mente innamorata, che donnea
con la mia donna sempre, di ridure
ad essa li occhi più che mai ardea:
e se natura o arte fè pasture
da pigliare occhi, per aver la mente,
in carne umana o nelle sue pitture,
tutte adunate, parebber niente
ver lo piacer divin che mi refulse,
quando mi volsi al suo viso ridente.
E la virtù che lo sguardo m'indulse,

del bel nido di Leda mi divelse,
e nel ciel velocissimo m'impulse.

42. *Pur.* XVI, 85.

43. *Conv.* IV, xii, 16–18.

II: *Dante's Conception of Poetic Expression*

1. C. S. Singleton, "Dante's Allegory," *Speculum*, XXV (1950), 78–86 (reprinted in his *Dante Studies I—Commedia: Elements of Structure* [Cambridge, Mass., 1954]); Bruno Nardi, "Le figurazioni allegoriche e l'allegoria della 'donna gentile' " and "I sensi delle Scritture" in his *Nel mondo di Dante* (Roma, 1944), 23–40, 55–61. See also Nardi's "Dante profeta," in his *Dante e la cultura medievale*, 336–416, esp. 375 ff. For medieval discussions of allegory and modern studies on Dante's view see *Il Convivio*, ed. G. Busnelli and G. Vandelli, I (1953), 240–242.

2. *Conv.* II, i, 2–9. The English translation is from that by Philip H. Wicksteed (London, 1903), 63–64.

Dico che, sì come nel primo capitolo è narrato, questa sposizione conviene essere litterale e allegorica. E a ciò dare a intendere, si vuol sapere che le scritture si possono intendere e deonsi esponere massimamente per quattro sensi. L'uno si chiama litterale, [e questo è quello che non si stende più oltre che la lettera de le parole fittizie, sì come sono le favole de li poeti. L'altro si chiama allegorico] e questo è quello che si nasconde sotto 'l manto di queste favole, ed è una veritade ascosa sotto bella menzogna: sì come quando dice Ovidio che Orfeo facea con la cetera mansuete le fiere, e li arbori e le pietre a sè muovere; che vuol dire che lo savio uomo con lo strumento de la sua voce fa[r]ia mansuescere e umiliare li crudeli cuori, e fa[r]ia muovere a la sua volontade coloro che non hanno vita di scienza e d'arte: e coloro che non hanno vita ragionevole alcuna sono quasi come pietre. E perchè questo nascondimento fosse trovato per li savi, nel penultimo trattato si mosterrà. Veramente li teologi questo senso prendono altrimenti che li poeti; ma però che mia intenzione è qui lo modo de li poeti seguitare, prendo lo senso allegorico secondo che per li poeti è usato.

Lo terzo senso si chiama morale, e questo è quello che li lettori deono intentamente andare appostando per le scritture, ad utilitade di loro e di loro discenti: sì come appostare si può ne lo Evangelio, quando

Cristo salìo lo monte per transfigurarsi, che de li dodici Apostoli menò seco li tre; in che moralmente si può intendere che a le secretissime cose noi dovemo avere poca compagnia.

Lo quarto senso si chiama anagogico, cioè sovrasenso; e questo è quando spiritualmente si spone una scrittura, la quale ancora [sia vera] eziandio nel senso litterale, per le cose significate significa de le superne cose de l'etternal gloria, sì come vedere si può in quello canto del Profeta che dice che, ne l'uscita del popolo d'Israel d'Egitto, Giudea è fatta santa e libera. Chè avvegna essere vero secondo la lettera sia manifesto, non meno è vero quello che spiritualmente s'intende, cioè che ne l'uscita de l'anima dal peccato, essa sia fatta santa e libera in sua potestate.

3. Wicksteed (*op. cit.*, 67 n.) feels that in spite of what Dante actually says he is distinguishing between the two allegories primarily by the difference from the literal sense.

4. *Il Convivio*, ed. Busnelli and Vandelli, 241–242.

5. *Nel mondo di Dante*, 55–61.

6. On allegory and related subjects in the Middle Ages, Edgar De Bruyne's work supersedes all others. I have drawn heavily on his *Etudes d'esthétique médiévale*, I, 339 ff.; II, 302 ff. The usual allegorical scheme of the theologians was first clearly worked out by Cassian, *Collationes* XIV, 8; *P.L.*, 49: cols 962B–965B. He uses *sensus tropologicus* instead of *sensus moralis* for the second meaning of a text, a meaning which applies to human character. His *sensus allegoricus* is also called *mysticus* and is the third sense, *not* the second, referring to prophecies in the Old Testament. An elaborate allegorical or "mystical" reading of the book of nature, with the realities of nature taken as a system of divine symbols, was developed early in Rhabanus Maurus' *Allegoriae in universam sacram scripturam; P.L.*, 112: cols. 849 sq. This conception, in simpler form, is the basis of Cassian's fourth—anagogical—sense, in which realities refer to eternal truths. But between Cassian and Rhabanus "allegorical" and "mystical" shifted their reference from prophetic truths in Scripture to the transcendental meanings of things and events in Scripture and nature.

Karl Vossler pointed out that religious texts were interpreted primarily in the anagogical sense, history in the moral sense, and poetry in its allegorical or conceptual meaning. A relatively late development in allegorical theory, this indicates a further shift in the reference and meaning of the word allegorical. It refers in this scheme to the second sense. Vossler, however, does not make the traditional distinctions between allegorical interpretations of sacred and profane texts. Profane texts could have only one other level besides the literal whether that level revealed moral or conceptual truths (*Die göttliche Komödie* [Heidelberg, 1925], I, 143).

The question of allegory is complex and confusing because allegory served a variety of purposes. In reference to Scripture and the writings of the pagans, the allegorical method was used to save the morality of parts of certain works or to adapt primitive and naïve elements of religious tradition for more sophisticated minds. This mode of allegory seems to have begun when Theagenes (sixth century B.C.), moved by piety, allegorized Homer in order to make his gods acceptable to a different religious consciousness. Philo applied the technique for the same reason, and for philosophical reasons as well, to the Old Testament. The method later became popular among the Alexandrian fathers. (For an excellent outline of the varieties of multiple interpretation see Harry Caplan, "The Four Senses of Scriptural Interpretation and the Medieval Theory of Preaching," *Speculum*, IV [1929], 282–290.)

But there is a great difference between the kind of allegorizing which derives from the ethical or philosophic impulse, the kind that emerges when rationalism and morality confront the creations of the poetic consciousness, and the allegorizing of nature and history made possible by Christian metaphysics. The providence of a personal God who ruled the universe gave new typological meaning to events in the universal plan, and the analogical relationship which Christian thought came to posit between the Creator and the creature formed the basis of a metaphysics of cosmic allegory wherein the created world was conceived as an image of the Creator. Of course, these conceptions of allegory were all interfused, so that the impulse to save the morality of sacred and profane writings was present even when interpreters worked within the framework of the metaphysics of allegory.

7. De Bruyne, *op. cit.*, II, 310 ff.; Joseph A. Mazzeo, "Universal Analogy and the Culture of the Renaissance," *JHI*, XV (1954), 299–304, 302.

8. *Dantis Alagherii epistolae; The Letters of Dante*, trans. and ed. Paget Toynbee (Oxford, 1920), *Ep*. X, 7 and 8, 134 ff. Translations and citations from the letters are from this edition.

Ad evidentiam itaque dicendorum, sciendum est quod istius operis non est simplex sensus, immo dici potest *polysemos*, hoc est plurium sensuum; nam primus sensus est qui habetur per literam, alius est qui habetur per significata per literam. Et primus dicitur literalis, secundus vero allegoricus, sive mysticus. Qui modus tractandi, ut melius pateat, potest considerari in his versibus: "In exitu Israel de Aegypto, domus Iacob de populo barbaro, facta est Iudaea sanctificatio eius, Israel potestas eius." Nam si ad literam solam inspiciamus, significatur nobis exitus filiorum Israel de Aegypto, tempore Moysis; si ad allegoriam, nobis significatur nostra redemptio facta per Christum; si ad moralem sensum, significatur nobis conversio animae de luctu et miseria peccati ad statum gratiae; si ad anagogicum, significatur exitus animae sanctae ab huius corruptionis servitute ad aeternae gloriae libertatem. Et quamvis isti sensus mystici variis appellentur nominibus, generaliter omnes dici possunt allegorici, quum sint a literali sive historiali diversi. Nam allegoria dicitur ab *alleon* graece, quod in latinum dicitur alienum, sive diversum.

His visis, manifestum est quod duplex oportet esse subiectum, circa quod currant alterni sensus. Et ideo videndum est de subiecto huius operis, prout ad literam accipitur; deinde de subiecto, prout allegorice sententiatur. Est ergo subiectum totius operis, literaliter tantum accepti, status animarum post mortem simpliciter sumptus. Nam de illo et circa illum totius operis versatur processus. Si vero accipiatur opus allegorice, subiectum est homo prout merendo et demerendo per arbitrii libertatem iustitiae praemiandi et puniendi obnoxius est.

9. *Nel mondo di Dante*, 60–61.

10. Singleton, *Dante Studies I*, 91.

11. *Il Convivio*, ed. Busnelli and Vandelli, 241.

12. *Dante Studies I*, viii.

13. *Ibid.*, 61. Singleton distinguishes between allegory and symbolism: "Symbolism is Dante's imitation of the structure of the real world, and allegory is his imitation of the structure of God's other book, Holy Scripture" (29). This is a fruitful distinction, although in medieval usage, at least after the time of Rhabanus Maurus, *res* meant a reality whether a thing or event. Both the book of nature and the book of Scripture (and, by extension, of history) were allegorical. It does clarify the question, however, if we reserve the term symbol for the meaning which inheres in a thing or object considered more or less in isolation and keep the term allegory—an extended metaphor or

analogy—for an integrated series of symbols or events. It is confusing to refer to an event as symbolic since it is composed of a plurality of elements extended in time.

14. On typological correspondences between individual and universal dramas of salvation see Jean Danielou, *The Bible and the Liturgy* (Notre Dame, Ind., 1956).

15. See Edmund Gardner, *Dante and the Mystics* (London, 1913), for the passages and doctrines referred to in the letter: ch. ii on St. Augustine, ch. iv on St. Bernard, and ch. v on Richard of St. Victor. On the impossibility of describing ultimate reality cf. *Paradiso* I, 4, 70; XXIV, 19; XXXI, 137.

16. *Ep.* X, 29, 570 ff.: Vidit ergo, ut dicit, aliqua "quae referre nescit et nequit rediens." Diligenter quippe notandum est quod dicit "nescit et nequit." Nescit quia oblitus, nequit quia, si recordatur et contentum tenet, sermo tamen deficit. Multa namque per intellectum videmus, quibus signa vocalia desunt; quod satis Plato insinuat in suis libris per assumptionem metaphorismorum, multa enim per lumen intellectuale vidit quae sermone proprio nequivit exprimere.

17. See above, Chapter I, n. 12.

18. St. Thomas Aquinas, *In Aristotelis librum De anima commentarium,* ed. P. F. A. M. Pirotta (3d ed.; Torino and Roma, 1948), I, lectio VIII, nn. 107–108.

19. *Ibid.*, I, lectio XII, n. 190.

20. *Ep.* X, 15, 267 ff., and 16, 271 ff: Quod finis totius et partis est, removere viventes in hac vita de statu miseriae, et perducere ad statum felicitatis. Genus philosophiae sub quo hic in tot et parte proceditur est morale negotium, sive ethica; quia non ad speculandum, sed ad opus inventum est totum et pars.

21. On the patristic and scholastic attacks against poetry and Dante's defense see Nancy Lenkeith, "The Poet as Prophet," in her *Dante and the Legend of Rome,* 33 ff. Miss Lenkeith points out that Dante applied to the poet concepts and formulas of theological prophecy like "dictation" and inspiration. Cf. Nardi, *Dante e la cultura,* 336–416. St. Thomas, with his usual distrust of imagery, values prophecy accomplished solely through the intellect over prophecy accomplished by imagination or images (*Summa theologiae* 2–2 q. 174 a. 4). E. R. Curtius bases Dante's claim of rivaling philosophy entirely on section 271 of the letter to Can Grande in which he discusses the "modes" of treatment or the "form" of the poem. Curtius observes that five of the

ten "modes" are poetic-rhetorical and five are philosophical. Dante's analysis of modes, however, is purely affirmative in character and neither explains why the poem gives truth nor defines its nature in terms of a general theory of linguistic expression (*European Literature and the Latin Middle Ages,* trans. W. R. Trask [London, 1953], 222–225, 480 ff.).

22. On medieval theories of dreams, prophecies, and visions see Nardi, *Dante e la cultura,* 295–301, 367 ff., and *Nel mondo di Dante,* 73 ff. He points out that dreams in Dante's psychology often reveal in sensible signs and images truths which cannot be revealed by pure reason. Revelation by way of dreams and visions may come through the direct action of incorporeal agents such as God and the angels or through corporeal agents such as heavenly bodies (e.g., *Conv.* II, vii, 8–13). Thus in *Purgatorio* XVII, 13, the light that enters the "immaginativa" comes from the heavens themselves or through the volition of one who sends it down.

23. Peter Abelard, *Introductio ad theologiam* I, 19; *P.L.,* 178: col. 1021C sq. Cf. col. 1022C and 1023B where he refers to Macrobius' use of metaphor for the same purpose.

24. Maurice de Gandillac, *Oeuvres complètes du pseudo-Denys l'Aréopagite* (Paris, 1943), Introduction, 28–29.

25. Dionysius, *Ep.* IX, 1; *P.G.,* 3: col. 1105D.

26. Gandillac, *op. cit.,* Introduction, 31, 35 n. 3; Dionysius, *Th. myst.* I, 1; *P.G.,* 3: col. 97B. The light which is Cacciaguida's smile (*Par.* XVII, 34) both hides and reveals him in a manner analogous to the operation of metaphor and symbolism in Dionysius' theory:

> Ma per chiare parole e con preciso
> latin rispuose quello amor paterno,
> chiuso e parvante del suo proprio riso.

Dionysius also held that another purpose of allegory is to protect sacred matter from profane consideration, a viewpoint deriving not from his speculations on the nature of expression but from the traditions of secret initiation.

27. Dionysius, *Div. nom.* IV, 13; *P.G.,* 3: col. 712A.

28. *Ep.* IX, 1; *P.G.,* 3: col. 1108B.

29. *Coel. hier.* I; *P.G.,* 3: col. 124A.

30. *Eccles. hier.* II, 3, 3; *P.G.,* 3: cols. 397D–400A; *Eccles. hier.* VII, 3, 5; *P.G.,* 3: col. 560B.

31. *Idem.* The Dionysian theory of symbolical and dialectical theory

appears again in Tasso's *Discorsi del poema eroico*, Bk. II. He maintained that both mystical theologians and poets worked in the symbolic mode, a nobler one than the dialectical. Thus mystical theologians and poets have a higher form of expression than philosophers.

32. *Par.* IV, 37–63:

> Qui si mostraron, non perchè sortita
> sia questa spera lor, ma per far segno
> della celestial c'ha men salita.
> Così parlar conviensi al vostro ingegno,
> però che solo da sensato apprende
> ciò che fa poscia d'intelletto degno.
> Per questo la Scrittura condescende
> a vostra facultate, e piedi e mano
> attribuisce a Dio, ed altro intende;
> e Santa Chiesa con aspetto umano
> Gabriel e Michel vi rappresenta,
> e l'altro che Tobia rifece sano.
> Quel che Timeo dell'anime argomenta
> non è simile a ciò che qui si vede,
> però che, come dice, par che senta.
> Dice che l'alma alla sua stella riede,
> credendo quella quindi esser decisa
> quando natura per forma la diede;
> e forse sua sentenza è d'altra guisa
> che la voce non suona, ed esser puote
> con intenzion da non esser derisa.
> S'elli intende tornare a queste ruote
> l'onor della influenza e 'l biasmo, forse
> in alcun vero suo arco percuote.
> Questo principio, male inteso, torse
> già tutto il mondo quasi, sì che Giove,
> Mercurio e Marte a nominar trascorse.

33. Thomas Whittaker, *The Neo-Platonists* (Cambridge, Eng., 1928), 193.

34. *Par.* XXXIII, 106:

> Omai sarà più corta mia favella,
> pur a quel ch'io ricordo, che d'un fante
> che bagni ancor la lingua alla mammella.
> Non perchè più ch'un semplice sembiante

> fosse nel vivo lume ch'io mirava,
> che tal è sempre qual s'era davante;
> ma per la vista che s'avvalorava
> in me guardando, una sola parvenza,
> mutandom'io, a me si travagiava.

35. *Par.* XXIII, 61:

> E così, figurando il paradiso,
> convien saltar lo sacrato poema,
> come chi trova suo cammin riciso.

The fiction of the poem, as Mr. Singleton maintains, is that it literally happened and that it therefore must be understood as imitative of theological allegory or metaphor; nevertheless we are confronted by the apparent anomalies such as *Inferno* IX, 61 ff., or even the first two cantos of the poem, where we seem to be in the world of poetic allegory proper. In other words, Dante sometimes seems to ask us to look beyond an event for its meaning. Such exceptions may be more apparent than real, since Dante's poetic "veil" is never presented to us as a simple fiction made for the sake of its abstract meaning alone.

III: Dante's Conception of Love and Beauty

1. St. Thomas Aquinas, *Summa theologiae* 1, q. 60 a. 1.
2. *Ibid.*, 1, q. 102 a. 2 ad 2.
3. St. Augustine, *De civ. Dei* XI, 28; *P.L.*, 41: col. 342.
4. St. Augustine, *Conf.* XIII, 9; *P.L.*, 32: cols. 848–849. Cf. the general introduction to the *Obras de San Agustin*, by P. Victorino Capanaga, I (2d ed.; Madrid, 1950), 66 ff., for a discussion of this doctrine of *amor* as *pondus*. In the *De Trinitate* (X, 1, 3; *P.L.*, 42: col. 474) St. Augustine relates love to knowledge. Love follows upon knowing, but it is a desire to know more. Because a man loves what he knows, he desires to know what he does not yet know. Knowledge generates love which in turn demands more knowledge and so on in a spiral. Such a pattern of circularity is an important motif in the *Paradiso* in which increase of knowledge generates love and this in turn demands more knowledge.
5. Boethius, *Consolatio philosophiae* III, metrum 9, 18–25, in *Boethius, The Theological Tractates, The Consolation of Philosophy*, by H. F. Stewart and E. K. Rand (London and Cambridge, Mass.,

1918). The poem cited is an excellent paraphrase of the first part of the *Timaeus.*

6. *Consolatio philosophiae* III, metrum 2, 34–38.

7. *De intelligentiis*, LII, ed. by Clemens Baeumker in *Witelo.*

8. *Conv.* III, ii, 3–9. According to Bruno Nardi, love in Dante's *Convivio* is no longer a "disio che vien dal core" as in the *Vita nuova*, but a *virtus unitiva*, a notion which Dante may have derived from Dionysius (*De div. nom.* IV, 12, 15, 17) and which is a neoplatonic definition of love. This idea coupled with Boethius' notion of *mentibus hominum veri boni naturaliter inserta cupiditas* (*Cons.* III, pr. 2 and 3) is, according to Nardi, the source of the dialectic of the love passage in *Convivio* IV, xii, 14–19, and the "Esce di man" passage in *Purgatorio* XVI, 85–93. For Boethius this inborn natural desire to return to the Creator which exists even in animals is a vague sentiment, existing in the manner of a dream, of their origin and their goal (*Cons.* III, pr. 8). Nardi also traces the idea of the natural motion of the soul to God in *Convivio* III, ii, 4–7, to the *Liber de causis* (Bruno Nardi, *Dante e la cultura medievale*, 47–55).

9. *Conv.* III, iii, 2–5.

10. *Conv.* III, iii, 6–7, 9–13.

11. *Conv.* IV, xii, 14–17. For one form of the subjective ladder of love cf. *Convivio* IV, xxii, 4–8, where Dante expounds the various forms of self-love culminating, through purification, in the love of the highest or intellectual self. The natural appetite of the mind which the Greeks call *hormen* is infused in us from the source of our generation by divine grace. At first it seems like the ordinary forms of appetition, the purely natural forms. Later, however, it differentiates itself from them, in a manner similar to the way in which various grains look alike at first but change and differ as they grow. So all animals, rational and dumb, begin by behaving alike in their basic self-love which is physical in nature and necessary for survival. There is, later on, a differentiation between the appetite of men and of dumb animals and, in the human species, between the various forms and directions which this self-love may take. If this self-love of humans takes the right path, it eventually culminates in love of the best part of the self, the intellect, and in the life of contemplation of God, in this life only through his effects, in the afterlife directly.

12. *Par.* XXXIII, 55:

Da quinci innanzi il mio veder fu maggio
che 'l parlar nostro, ch'a tal vista cede,
e cede la memoria a tanto oltraggio.

Qual è colui che somniando vede,
che dopo il sogno la passione impressa
rimane, e l'altro alla mente non riede,
cotal son io, chè quasi tutta cessa
mia visione, ed ancor mi distilla
nel core il dolce, che nacque da essa.

13. *Par.* XXXIII, 91:

La forma universal di questo nodo
credo ch'i'vidi, perchè più di largo,
dicendo questo, mi sento ch'i'godo.

Un punto solo m'è maggior letargo
che venticinque secoli alla 'mpresa,
che fè Nettuno ammirar l'ombra d'Argo.

14. *Par.* XXIII, 40:

Come foco di nube si diserra
per dilatarsi sì che non vi cape,
e fuor di sua natura in giù s'atterra,
la mente mia così, tra quelle dape
fatta più grande, di sè stessa usciò,
e che si fesse rimembrar non sape.
"Apri li occhi e riguarda qual son io:
tu hai vedute cose, che possente
se' fatto a sostener lo riso mio."
Io era come quei che si risente
di visione oblita e che s'ingegna
indarno di ridurlasi alla mente,
quand'io udi' questa proferta, degna
di tanto grato, che mai non si stingue
del libro che 'l preterito rassegna.

15. *Pur.* XVI, 85:

Esce di mano a lui che la vagheggia
prima che sia, a guisa di fanciulla
che piangendo e ridendo pargoleggia,
l'anima semplicetta che sa nulla,
salvo che, mossa da lieto fattore,
volentier torna a ciò che la trastulla.

Di picciol bene in pria sente sapore;
    quivi s'inganna, e dietro ad esso corre,
    se guida o fren non torce suo amore
Onde convenne legge per fren porre;
    convenne rege aver che discernesse
    dalla vera città almen la torre.

16. *Par.* VII, 130:

Li angeli, frate, e 'l paese sincero
    nel qual tu se', dir si posson creati,
    sì some sono, in loro essere intero;
ma li elementi che tu hai nomati
    e quelle cose che di lor si fanno
    da creata virtù sono informati.
Creata fu la materia ch'elli hanno;
    creata fu la virtù informante
    in queste stelle che 'ntorno a lor vanno.
L'anima d'ogne bruto e delle piante
    di complession potenziata tira
    lo raggio e 'l moto delle luci sante;
ma vostra vita sanza mezzo spira
    la somma beninanza, e la innamora
    di sè sì che poi sempre la disira.

17. Nancy Lenkeith refers to *De vera religione* (*P.L.*, 34: cols. 123 sq.) as a possible source for Dante's version of love nostalgia, although she acknowledges that the explicit statement that the soul comes forth from God is lacking in the passage in question and that it is present in Petrarch's allusion to the Augustinian passage to be found in the *Secretum*, I. She also points out that the purification of the soul from sense, necessary so that the soul can wake from the sleep which makes it forget its first splendor and its Creator, is a description of the mystic way. It is not the use of creatures to ascend to God but a purely subjective process of progressive purification of the love uniting the individual with God (Nancy Lenkeith, *Dante and the Legend of Rome*, 47-48).

I cannot suggest an explicit source, but the Boethian notions of the outgoing and return of all things from and to God and of the implanted desire for the Supreme Good whose attainment is happiness suggest a possible context. Boethius, in the *Consolatio*, also expounds the notion that men are deceived by lesser goods and seek to amass them, ignorant of their true goal (II, pr. 2). In the passage which affords the closest parallel to Dante, even to the extent of adopting a dream image, he says: "Vos quoque, o terrena animalia, tenui licet imagine vestrum tamen principium somniatis verumque illum beatitudinis finem licet minime perspici qualicumque tamen cogitatione prospicitis eoque vos ad verum bonum naturalis ducit intentio et ab eodem multiplex error abducit. Considera namque an per ea quibus se homines adepturos beatitudinem putant ad destinatum finem valeant pervenire" (III, pr. 3). All of the elements of the divine origin of the soul, its implanted desire to return to its Creator, the restless, unconscious pursuit of a half-forgotten Supreme Good through lesser goods, the image of the dream, are present in Boethius. Dante describes the recollection of God as the imprinted passion of a dream that is over, and Boethius describes it as a kind of actual dream state. Boethius emphasizes how men err by remaining fixed in their desire on some finite rung in the hierarchy of objects of desire, and Dante emphasizes a more positive sense of the *use* of creatures to attain the Supreme Good. It is rather a question of emphasis than of difference.

18. *Pur.* XVIII, 19:

> L'animo, ch'è creato ad amar presto,
>> ad ogni cosa è mobile che piace,
>> tosto che dal piacere in atto è desto.
> Vostra apprensiva da esser verace
>> tragge intenzione, e dentro a voi si spiega,
>> sì che l'animo ad essa volger face;
> e se, rivolto, inver di lei si piega,
>> quel piegare è amor, quell'è natura
>> che per piacer di novo in voi si lega.

It is important to remember that for Dante as for St. Bernard certain ideas are not to be reached except through love and its maturing flame (*Par.* VII, 20). The notion rests on the idea that beauty is a harmony and the most excellent harmony is that of the virtues. To know the virtues is to have pleasure and to acquire thereby the desire of practicing them. This desire, or love, restrains the passions, breaks up vicious habits, and gives rise to internal happiness of the kind which must necessarily accompany the proper activity of the soul.

19. *Pur.* XVIII, 28:

> Poi, come 'l foco movesi in altura

> per la sua forma ch'è nata a salire
> là dove più in sua matera dura,
> così l'animo preso entra in disire,
> ch'è moto spiritale, e mai non posa
> fin che la cosa amata li fa gioire.

On the "binding" of the will in loving cf. St. Thomas Aquinas, *Summa theologiae* 1–2, q. 10 a. 2; 1–2, q. 26 a. 3; 1–2, q. 77 a. 2.

20. *Pur.* XVIII, 55:

> Però, là onde vegna lo intelletto
> delle prime notizie, omo non sape,
> e de' primi appetibili l'affetto,
> che sono in voi, sì come studio in ape
> di far lo mele; e questa prima voglia
> merto di lode o di biasmo non cape.

> Or perchè a questa ogn'altra si raccoglia,
> innata v'è la virtù che consiglia,
> e dell'assenso de' tener la soglia.

> Quest'è il principio là onde si piglia
> ragion di meritare in voi, secondo
> che buoni e rei amori accoglie e viglia.

> Color che ragionando andaro al fondo
> s'accorser d'esta innata libertate;
> però moralità lasciaro al mondo.

> Onde, poniam che di necessitate
> surga ogni amor che dentro a voi s'accende,
> di ritenerlo è in voi la podestate.

> La nobile virtù Beatrice intende
> per lo libero arbitrio, e però guarda
> che l'abbi a mente, s'a parlar ten prende.

21. St. Thomas Aquinas, *Summa theologiae* 1–2, q. 26 a. 1.

22. *Ibid.*, 1–2, q. 26 a. 2.

23. The Aristotelian doctrine of *complacentia* was used to formulate conceptually the Provençal conceit that the immediate perception of one's lady was a prerequisite to the birth of love. Love comes into being *upon* the eyes of the lady when encountered by those of her future lover. The love thus generated is conveyed on bright beams of *light* from her eyes to his. It passes through them to take up its abode in his heart. Cf. *Vita nuova* XX, sonnet 10.

Amore e 'l cor gentil sono una cosa,
Siccom'il Saggio in suo dittato pone;
E così esser l'un senza l'altro osa,
Com'alma razional senza ragione.
Fagli natura, quando è amorosa,
Amor per sire, e 'l cor per sua magione,
Dentro alla qual dormendo si riposa
Talvolta poca, e tal lunga stagione.
Beltate appare in saggia donna pui
che piace agli occhi sì, che dentro al core
Nasce un desio della cosa piacente:
E tanto dura talora in costui,
Che fa svegliar lo spirito d'Amore;
E simil face in donna uomo valente.

Cf. also sections XIX, XXI, XXVI.

24. St. Thomas Aquinas, *Summa theologiae* 1, q. 75 a. 6.

25. *Conv.* III, viii, 3–5, esp. 5.

26. *Par.* XXIV, 1:

"O sodalizio eletto alla gran cena
del benedetto Agnello, il qual vi ciba
sì, che la vostra viglia è sempre piena,
se per grazia di Dio questi preliba
di quel che cade della vostra mensa,
prima che morte tempo li prescriba,
ponete mente all'affezione immensa,
e roratelo alquanto: voi bevete
sempre del fonte onde vien quel ch'ei pensa."

The goal and dialectical nature of love is also expressed in the image of a "sweet fruit" sought through the boughs of a tree. There is almost certainly an allusion to the "tree" of Porphyry, the diagram illustrating the logical and ontological structure of reality, a commonplace in medieval teaching of logic. *Pur.* XXVII, 115:

"Quel dolce pome che per tanti rami
cercando va la cura de'mortali,
oggi porrà in pace le tue fami."
Virgilio inverso me queste cotali
parole usò.

" 'That sweet fruit which the care of mortals goes to seek on so

many boughs shall today give peace to thy cravings.' Such were
Virgil's words to me."

Porphyry's tree is a representation of the scale of forms, and according to the fundamental principle of Greek idealistic thought every
higher form contains virtually whatever belongs to the lower, i.e.,
repeats the lower on a higher level while transcending it. Thus Virgil
says of spiritual love what Francesca had said of carnal love in *Inferno*
V, 103 ff. *Pur.* XXII, 10:

> quando Virgilio incominciò: "Amore
>   acceso di virtù, sempre altro accese,
>   pur che la fiamma sua paresse fore . . ."

". . . when Virgil began: 'Love kindled by virtue always kindles
another, if only its flame appear without . . .' "

27. On this subject see H. O. Taylor, *The Classical Heritage of the
Middle Ages* (New York, 1903), 123 ff.; Edouard Krakowski,
L'Esthétique de Plotin et son influence (Paris, 1929), 187–208. A recent
study on all aspects of classical culture in the Middle Ages with an
excellent bibliography on medieval platonism is Paul Renucci, *L'Aven-
ture de l'humanisme européen au moyen-age (IVe–XIVe siècle)*
(Paris, 1953). See also Karel Svoboda, *L'Esthétique de saint Augustin
et ses sources* (Paris, 1933); Emmanuel Chapman, *Saint Augustine's
Philosophy of Beauty* (New York, 1939).

28. Plotinus, *Ennead* I, 6, for the nature of beauty. For Plotinus'
"sermon" on beauty with Plato's *Phaedrus* myth as a text see *Ennead*
V, 8. In this discourse he calls light supremely beautiful. For the
discourse on love see *Ennead* III, 5. I have used the edition and translation of Emile Brehier, *Plotin: Enneades* (6 v.; Paris, 1924–1938).

29. St. Augustine, *De civ. Dei* XI, 27, 2; *P.L.*, 41: col. 341.

30. St. Augustine, *De Trin.* XV, 12, 21; *P.L.*, 42: col. 1075: Sed
absit a nobis ut ea quae per sensus corporis didicimus vera esse
dubitemus: per eos quippe didicimus caelum et terram. Et ea quae in
eis nota sunt nobis, quantum ille qui et nos et ipsa condidit, innotescere
nobis voluit.

31. St. Augustine, *De vera religione* 18, 35; *P.L.*, 34: col. 137: Ergo
ex Deo est etiam minima species. Sane quod de specie, hoc etiam de
forma dici potest. Neque enim frustra tam speciosissimum, quam etiam
formosissimum in laude ponitur.

32. St. Augustine, *De vera religione* 20, 40; *P.L.*, 34: cols. 138–139:

Notes to III: Love and Beauty

Ita omnis corporea creatura, si tantummodo possideatur ab anima quae diligit Deum, bonum est infimum, et in genere suo pulchrum, quoniam forma et specie continetur.

33. Edgar De Bruyne, *Etudes d'esthétique médiévale*, III, 101; II, 80 ff.

34. St. Augustine, *De Trin.* VI, 10, 12; *P.L.*, 42: col. 932.

35. *De Trin.* VI, 10, 11; *P.L.*, 42: col. 931. Cf. Etienne Gilson, *Introduction a l'étude de saint Augustin* (2d ed.; Paris, 1943), 279 ff. In speaking of the perfect resemblance between the Son and the Father St. Augustine adds that God is the first species (*prima species*) by which all things are constituted in their respective species (*qua sunt . . . speciate . . . omnia*) and the form by which all things possess their form (*qua sunt . . . formata . . . omnia*). The similitude of the Son to the Father is a special kind, for he is the Word, the exemplar of all things. All beings except the Son possess similitude by virtue of participation in him and therefore in some part are dissimilar to what they resemble, whether it is God or some other thing. The Son as his own exemplar is similitude itself, and there can be no dissimilarity between him and the Father of whom he is the similitude. St. Augustine here is using the words *forma* and *species* primarily in their ontological reference. But it is precisely this perfect similitude to pattern which engenders beauty, and that meaning, although not explicit, is not absent (*De diversis quaestionibus* LXXXIII, quest. 23; *P.L.*, 40: cols. 16–17).

36. Another instance of the way in which Augustine handles the multiple meanings of *forma* and *species* occurs in *De civitate Dei* (XVII, 16, 1; *P.L.*, 41; col. 549) when St. Augustine comments on the method of interpretation of Scripture in reference to Psalm 14: 1–9. He says that those who acknowledge Christ as king should inquire into the various metaphorical or tropological meanings of the Psalm. They would then find that Christ's form is beautiful (*speciosus*) beyond the beauty of men, with a beauty which is more to be admired and loved the less it is a corporeal beauty. Here the term *speciosus* is used to refer to the beauty of Christ's form, a higher form of beauty because it is less corporeal.

37. *Enarr. in Psal.* 144 n. 13; *P.L.*, 37: col. 1878.

Stanislao Prato, in his article "Essenza ed immagini simboliche della luce e delle tenebre confermate da vari passi della 'Divina Commedia' e specialmente del 'Paradiso'" (*Giornale dantesco*, XIII [1905], 199–

236), pointed out that a philological study of various languages, Oriental as well as European, shows the primitive and profoundly rooted connection between the concept of beauty and light. Beauty as light also was felt to possess "revealing" powers and was conceived as a kind of mute language (215). Thus hell is a place where the sun does not shine and so is "silent" (*Inf.* I, 60), not "speaking" through its luminous beauty. Hell is also a place where all light is mute (*Inf.* V, 28). St. Augustine's notion of the revealing power of beauty as the mute voice of the Creator is simply a conceptualization and elaboration of this fundamental sense of the function of beauty.

38. St. Augustine, *Conf.* VII, 7; *P.L.*, 32: col. 744.
39. St. Augustine, *De quantitate animae* 1, 2; *P.L.*, 32: col. 1037.
40. Cf. Charles Boyer, *Sant'Agostino* (Milan, 1946), 127.
41. St. Augustine, *De vera religione* 39, 72; *P.L.*, 34: col. 154.
42. St. Augustine, *De civ. Dei* VIII, 6; *P.L.*, 41: cols. 231–232.

The ladder of beauty was a recurrent motif in St. Augustine's thought and was fully developed in his early dialogue *De quantitate animae*, a work which Dante referred to in the letter to Can Grande for authority in his claim to having had a supernatural vision. St. Augustine posits seven steps (*gradus*) which the soul must climb in order to perfect itself and attain beatitude. These are described in various parallel ways: psychologically, ontologically, and aesthetically. The process of ascent is based on the notion of the self-transcendence of spirit, consciousness taking successively higher and higher attitudes toward the natures which it comprehends and includes until it finds God. It begins by considering its relations toward corporeality, then turns in upon itself, and finally turns to God. Each phase of this activity reveals a new and higher kind of beauty so that the soul acts "beautifully concerning something else," "beautifully through something else," "beautifully about something else," "beautifully in the presence of something beautiful," "beautifully in something beautiful," "beautifully in the presence of Beauty," "beautifully in Beauty."

If we compare these two versions, late and early, of the ladder of beauty, we can see how much thought St. Augustine put into the question. Instead of the simple parallels of *De quantitate animae*, we have later a carefully worked out metaphysics of beauty (St. Augustine, *De quantitate animae* 35, 79; *P.L.*, 32: col. 1079). Cf. E. K. Rand, *Founders of the Middle Ages* (Cambridge, Mass., 1928), 251–284; Edmund Gardner, *Dante and the Mystics* (London, 1913), 45 ff. As early as the *Soliloquies* St. Augustine has predicated light and beauty of God as well as good and truth, without, however, working out the relationship between these predicates as he did later (*Soliloquiorum libri duo* I, 1–3; *P.L.*, 32: cols. 869–870).

43. De Bruyne, *op. cit.*, II, ch. v, 203 ff., esp. 208–218; III, 88 ff.

44. St. Augustine, *De natura boni* 3; *P.L.*, 42: col. 553: Nos enim catholici christiani Deum colimus, a quo omnia bona sunt, seu magna seu parva; a quo est omnis modus, a quo omnis ordo, seu magnus seu parvus.

45. De Bruyne, *op. cit.*, III, 88 ff.; Alexander of Hales, *Universae theologiae summa* II, q. 14, *membrum 1* and *resolutio*, Venice, 1576: Cum enim tria insint creaturae, modus, species et ordo, species maxime videtur illud esse secundum quod determinatur pulchritudo.

What this emphasis means he tells us in the following passage: Veritas est dispositio ex parte formae relata ad interius, pulchritudo est dispositione ex parte formae relata ad exterius: solebamus enim pulchrum dicere quod in se habebat unde conveniens esset in aspectu.

46. Robert Grosseteste, *De luce*, in *Die philosophischen Werke des Robert Grosseteste*, ed. Ludwig Baur (Baeumker's *Beiträge zur Geschichte der Philosophie des Mittelalters*, Band IX; Münster, 1912), 56.

47. Grosseteste, *De unica forma omnium*, ed. Baur, 108: Deus igitur est perfectio perfectissima, completio completissima, forma formosissima et species speciosissima.

48. St. Bonaventura, *Itinerarium mentis ad Deum* 1, 2, in *Tria opuscula seraphici doctoris S. Bonaventurae* (5th ed., Quaracchi, 1938): Cum enim secundum statum conditionis nostrae ipsa rerum universitas sit scala ad ascendendum in Deum.

49. St. Bonaventura, *Breviloquium* I, 6, 3, in *Tria opuscula:* Summe unum est summe primum, quia caret omne inceptione; et quia summe verum est summe aequale et pulchrum; et quia summe bonum est summe utile et proficium.

50. St. Bonaventura, *Breviloquium*, prologus, 3, 3: Est enim pulchritudo magna in machina mundana, sed longe maior in Ecclesia pulchritudine sanctorum charismatorum adornata, maxima autem in Ierusalem superna, supermaxima autem in illa Trinitate summa et beatissima. Cf. *Sermones de tempore, Dominica in Albus, Sermo* I 2 (Quaracchi ed., IX, 290), in which St. Bonaventura speaks of the luminous beauty of the heavens proclaiming their Creator and of

the manner in which the lure of the beauty of creatures leads to God.

51. St. Bonaventura, *Itinerarium* 1, 14.

52. *Ibid.*, 2, 7–8.

53. St. Bonaventura, *The Life of St. Francis,* 9, 1, trans. by E. Gurney Salter in the "Everyman" edition of *The Little Flowers, The Mirror of Perfection, and The Life of St. Francis,* introd. by Thomas Okey (London, 1910), 358.

54. Cf. on light metaphysics and poetics De Bruyne, *op. cit.,* III, 9 ff., where other references are given.

55. De Bruyne, *op. cit.,* III, 14, 16, 22–23; cf. also II, 177.

56. Émile Legouis, *Défense de la poésie française a l'usage des lecteurs anglais* (Paris et Londres, 1912).

57. Guibert of Nogent, *De vita sua* I, 2; *P.L.,* 156: col. 840.

58. Nicholas of Cusa, in *Oeuvres choisies de Nicolas de Cues,* by Maurice de Gandillac (Paris, 1942), 462–463.

59. Guibert of Nogent, *De vita sua* I, 2; *P.L.,* 156: col. 839. Cf. De Bruyne, *op. cit.,* II, 199.

60. De Bruyne, *op. cit.,* III, 31–41.

61. St. Bernard, *Sermones in canticum canticorum, Sermo* XXV; *P.L.,* 183: cols. 901D–902A.

62. *Sermones in canticum canticorum, Sermo* LXXXV; *P.L.,* 183: col. 1193C.

63. *Conv.* III, viii, 3–4. Cf. also *Conv.* III, ii, 17–19, in which, speaking of the divine nature of the rational soul or mind, Dante says that mind can be predicated only of mankind and of divine substances. He cites Boethius as saying to Philosophy that God sent her into the minds of men and as saying to God that he creates all things according to the supernal archetype (*superno essemplo*), the beautiful world which he, supremely beautiful, carries in his mind. It is thus in the ideas of the divine mind, the archetypal forms, that Dante, following Boethius, places the source of created beauty.

64. *Conv.* III, viii, 11.

65. *Conv.* III, ii. 14.

66. *Conv.* III, viii, 6–9.

67. *Conv.* III, viii, 13–14.

IV: Dante and the Pauline Modes of Vision

1. 2 Cor. 12: 2–4. I cite, throughout this chapter, the English of the Authorized Version. The Vulgate has: Scio hominem in Christo ante

annos quatuordecim (sive in corpore nescio, sive extra corpus nescio, Deus scit), raptum hujusmodi usque ad tertium caelum. Et scio hujusmodi hominem (sive in corpore, sive extra corpus, nescio, Deus scit), quoniam raptus est in paradisum, et audivit arcana verba, quae non licet homini loqui.

2. St. Gregory Nazianzen, *Oratio XVIII, Theologica* II, c. xvii; *P.G.*, 36: cols. 47C, 49A.

3. 1 Cor. 13: 12. The Vulgate is: Videmus nunc per speculum in aenigmate, tunc autem facie ad faciem. Nunc cognosco ex parte; tunc autem cognoscam sicut et cognitus sum.

4. Rom. 1: 20. Vulgate: Invisibilia enim ipsius, a creatura mundi, per ea quae facta sunt, intellecta, conspiciuntur: sempiterna quoque ejus virtus, et divinitas.

5. Cf. St. Thomas Aquinas, who concurs with St. Augustine on this definition (*Summa theologiae* 2–2, q. 180 a. 3 ad 2): "(Utrum ad vitam contemplativam pertineant diversi actus.) Ad secundum dicendum quod sicut dicit glossa Augustini ibidem [*De Trin.* XIV, c. 6; *P.L.*, 42: col. 1076] *speculantes dicit a speculo, non a specula.* Videre autem aliquid per speculum est videre causam per effectum in quo eius similitudo relucet. Unde *speculatio* ad meditationem redici videtur." The word speculation thus derives from "mirror," not from "watchtower." This is the way of knowledge of God possible to fallen man who in order to see him needs a kind of mirror, the creatures which God created.

6. St. Gregory the Great, *Moralium libri sive expositio in librum b. Job* XVIII, 54, n. 89; *P.L.*, 76: col. 95A–B.

7. On this question see Dom Cuthbert Butler (*Western Mysticism* [2d ed.; London, 1927], 125–133), who argues that this passage represents an inconsistency in St. Gregory's thought on the question, and F. H. Dudden (*Gregory the Great* [2 v.; London, 1905], II, 313 ff.), who claims that eternal brightness does not mean God's essence.

8. *Moralium* XXXI, 101; *P.L.*, 76: col. 629A. Cf. Butler, *op. cit.*, 127 ff., for more references to the "cloudy" character of contemplation in the works of St. Gregory.

9. *Homiliarum in Ezechielem prophetam libri duo, Homilia* XIII, n. 30; *P.L.*, 76: col. 868C–D.

10. II cor. 5: 6–7. Vulgate: Audentes igitur semper, scientes quoniam dum sumus in corpore, peregrinamur a Domino. (Per fidem enim ambulamus, et non per speciem).

11. St. Gregory of Nyssa, *In canticum canticorum homiliae, Homilia*

Notes to IV: Pauline Modes

XII; *P.G.*, 44: col. 1025B. Cf. also Joseph Marechal, *Etudes sur la psychologie des mystiques* (2 v.; Paris-Bruxelles, 1937), II, 19 ff.

12. St. Augustine, *De genesi ad litteram* XII, c. 27 n. 55; *P.L.*, 34: col. 477; cited in *Enchiridion asceticum*, ed. M. J. Rouët de Journel and J. Dutilleul (4th ed.; Barcelona, 1947), n. 655.

13. *De genesi ad litteram* XII, c. 28, n. 56; *P.L.*, 34: col. 478; cited in *Enchiridion asceticum*, n. 656.

14. A few authorities maintain that St. Augustine had a change of mind on this question, but Dom Butler's review of the problem (*op. cit.*, 84 ff.) shows that they have misread certain other passages in St. Augustine.

15. Butler, *op. cit.*, 86, 84–85, and, for the whole treatment of St. Augustine's conception of the vision of God, 78–88. Butler points out that there is no question that St. Augustine's account of the visions of Paul and Moses runs against the mainstream of theological and mystical speculation: "St. Thomas's acceptance is due, it may safely be said, to his reverence for St. Augustine . . . and has been a source of embarrassment to St. Thomas's commentators" (84, n. 1).

16. *De quantitate animae* 33, 76; *P.L.*, 32: col. 1076. Paget Toynbee also cites this passage in elucidating Dante's allusion to this work in the letter to Can Grande: *Dantis Alagherii epistolae*, 193.

17. Cf. Butler, *op. cit.*, 59–60, 65, and St. Augustine, *The Greatness of the Soul* (*Ancient Christian Writers*, vol. IX), trans. Joseph M. Colleran (London, 1949), 214, n. 101.

18. St. Bernard, *Sermones in canticum canticorum*, Sermo XXXI, 2; *P.L.*, 183: col. 941: At talis visio non est vitae praesentis, sed in novissimis reservatur. . . . Non sapiens, non sanctus, non propheta videre illum, sicuti est, potest, aut potuit in corpore hoc mortali.

19. *Sermones in canticum canticorum*, Sermo XXXIV, 1; *P.L.*, 183: cols. 959–960. See Etienne Gilson, *La Théologie mystique de Saint Bernard* (Paris, 1947), 113 ff., for other references to St. Bernard's statements on this question.

20. *De consideratione* V, 2, 3; *P.L.*, 182: col. 749C. See Burch, *op. cit.*, 28–29, in his long introduction on St. Bernard's epistemology. Consideration and contemplation were often used interchangeably, although St. Bernard carefully distinguished the two. *Contemplatio* is certain and is the soul's unerring intuition or apprehension of truth. *Consideratio* is thought in the process of seeking earnestly, the mind searching for truth. However, as St. Bernard admits, the two terms

are used indifferently for one another in practice. See *De considera-tione* II, 2, 5; *P.L.*, 182: col. 745.

21. *De consideratione* V, 1, 1; *P.L.*, 182: cols. 787–789.

22. *De gratia contemplationis libri quinque, Benjamin major*, I, 6; *P.L.*, 196: col. 70B–C.

23. *Benjamin major* I, 6; *P.L.*, 196: col. 72B–C. Cf. *Benjamin major* IV, 18 (*P.L.*, 196: cols. 458D–459A), on mysteries of Trinity revealed in this form of contemplation.

24. *Benjamin major* V, 19; *P.L.*, 196: 192A–B.

25. *Adnotationes mysticae in Psalmos, Adnotatio in Psalmum II; P.L.*, 196: col. 271A–D. Although Richard does not take up the question of seeing God in his essence in this life in *Benjamin major*, he seems to deny the possibility there when, symbolizing God as the sun of heaven, he says that no one can see the high noon of that heavenly day while in this corruptible flesh, although he does not dare deny that some have seen its early morning (*Benjamin major* III, 10; *P.L.*, 196: col. 120B).

26. St. Thomas Aquinas, *Summa theologiae* 1, q. 12 a. 11. The references to St. Augustine are to the following, all in *P.L.* 34: *De Gen. ad litt.* XII, c. 26, col. 476; c. 27, col. 477; c. 28, col. 478; c. 34, col. 482; *De videndo Deo* in *Epistola* 147, c. 13, col. 610. St. Thomas treats this question in several other works, some of which I will discuss below: *Sent.* III, d. 27 q. 3 a. 1; d. 35 q. 2 a. 2; IV, d. 49 q. 2 a. 7; *De veritate* q. 10 a. 11; *In II Corinth.* c. 12 lectio 1; *Quodl.* I q. 1.

27. *Summa theologiae* 2-2, q. 180 a. 5. Cf. *Summa contra gentiles* Liber III, c. 47.

28. *Summa theologiae* 2-2, q. 173 a. 1.

29. *Ibid.*, 2-2, q. 174 a. 3.

30. *Ibid.*, 2-2, q. 174 a. 4.

31. *Ibid.*, 2-2, q. 175 a. 3 ad 1 and 2.

32. St. Thomas Aquinas, *in II Corinth.* c. 12, lectio 1.

33. *Summa theologiae* 2-2, q. 175 a. 2.

34. *Ibid.*, 2-2, q. 175 a. 2 ad 1.

35. *De veritate* q. XVIII a. 1.

36. *Ibid.*, q. XVIII a. 1 ad 1.

37. *Ibid.*

38. *Ibid.*

39. *Ibid.*, q. XVIII a. 1 ad 4.

40. *Ibid.*, q. XIII a. 2. Cf. also, on St. Paul's rapture, St. Thomas Aquinas, IV *Sent.* d. 49 q. 2 a. 7 ad 5.

41. *De veritate* q. XIII a. 3.

42. *Ep.* X, 28, 525 ff.: Et postquam dixit quod fuit in loco illo Paradisi per suam circumlocutionem, prosequitur dicens se vidisse aliqua quae recitare non potest qui descendit. Et reddit causam, dicens quod "quod intellectus in tantum profundat se" in ipsum desiderium suum, quod est Deus, "quod memoria sequi non potest." Ad quae intelligenta sciendum est, quod intellectus humanus in hac vita, propter connaturalitatem et affinitatem quam habet ad substantiam intellectualem separatam, quando elevatur, in tantum elevatur ut memoria post reditum deficiat, propter transcendisse humanum modum. Et hoc insinuatur nobis per Apostolum ad Corinthios loquentem, ubi dicit: "Scio hominem (sive in corpore, sive extra corpus, nescio, Deus scit), raptum usque ad tertium coelum, et audivit arcana verba, quae non licet homini loqui." Ecce, postquam humanam rationem intellectus ascensione transierat, quae extra se agerentur non recordabatur. Hoc etiam est insinuatum nobis in Matthaeo, ubi tres discipuli ceciderunt in faciem suam, nihil postea recitantes, quasi obliti. Et in Ezechiele scribitur: "Vidi et cecidi in faciem meam." Et ubi ista invidis non sufficiant, legant Richardum de sancto Victore in libro *De Contemplatione;* legant Bernardum in libro *De Consideratione;* legant Augustinum in libro *De Quantitate Animae*, et non invidebunt. Si vero in dispositionem elevationis tantae propter peccatum loquentis oblatrarent, legant Danielem, ubi et Nabuchodonosor invenient contra peccatores aliqua vidisse divinitus, oblivionique mandasse. Nam "Qui oriri solem suum facit super bonos et males, et pluit super iustos et iniustos," aliquando misericorditer ad conversionem, aliquando severe ad punitionem, plus et minus, ut vult, gloriam suam quantumcumque male viventibus manifestat.

The biblical references in this section of the letter to Can Grande are in their order as follows: II Cor. 12: 2–4, which Dante quotes in a truncated version; Matt. 17: 1–8; Ezek. 1: 28 (Vulg. 2: 1); Dan. 2: 3–5; Matt. 5: 45.

43. St. Augustine so frequently speaks of a *clear* vision of eternal truth that it would be very easy to take him as advocating the general possibility of a vision of God's essence, even if he is not doing so. See Butler, *op. cit.*, 49 ff., esp. 50–51.

44. *Inf.* II, 31:

> Ma io perchè venirvi? o chi 'l concede?
> Io non Enea, io non Paolo sono:
> ma degno a ciò nè io nè altri crede.
> Per che, se del venire io m'abbandono,
> temo che la venuta non sia folle.

45. *Par.* XV, 25:

> Sì pia l'ombra d'Anchise si porse,
> se fede merta nostra maggior musa,
> quando in Eliso del figlio s'accorse.
> "O sanguis meus, o superinfusa
> gratia Dei, sicut tibi cui
> bis unquam coeli ianua reclusa?"

46. *Par.* I, 70:

> Trasumanar significar per verba
> non si porìa; però l'essemplo basti
> a cui esperienza grazia serba.
> S'i'era sol di me quel che creasti
> novellamente, amor che 'l ciel governi,
> tu 'l sai, che col tuo lume mi levasti.

Note that Dante has transcended the state of vision possible to unfallen man. Aquinas says that contemplation is only a partial restoration of that vision. Clearly Dante is claiming a higher vision than the one St. Thomas calls contemplation. In the Thomistic scene, he could only be claiming to see God in his essence since that is the only sight higher than contemplation.

47. *Par.* II, 37:

> S'io era corpo, e qui non si concepe
> com'una dimensione altra patìo,
> ch'esser convien se corpo in corpo repe,
> accender ne dovrìa più il disio
> di veder quella essenza in che si vede
> come nostra natura e Dio s'unìo.
> Lì si vedrà ciò che tenem per fede,
> non dimostrato, ma fia per sè noto
> a guisa del ver primo che l'uom crede.

48. *Par.* XXVIII, 130:

> E Dionisio con tanto disio
> a contemplar questi ordini si mise,

che li nomò e distinse com'io.
Ma Gregorio da lui poi si divise;
onde, sì tosto come li occhi aperse
in questo ciel, di sè medesmo rise.
E se tanto secreto ver proferse
mortale in terra, non voglio ch'ammiri;
chè chi 'l vide, qua su liel discoperse
con altro assai del ver di questi giri.

49. See St. Thomas Aquinas, *In librum beati Dionysii de divinis nominibus expositio*, ed. C. Pera (Taurini-Romae, 1950), nn. 219, 249, 700, and the corresponding texts.

50. *Par.* XXX, 58.

51. Cf. *Benjamin Major* III, 9; *P.L.*, 196: col. 118D–119A.

52. *Par.* XXX, 88:

E sì come di lei bevve la gronda
delle palpebre mie, così mi parve
di sua lunghezza divenuta tonda.
Poi come gente stata sotto larve
che pare altro che prima, se si sveste
la sembianza non sua in che disparve,
così mi si cambiaro in maggior feste
li fiori e le faville, sì ch'io vidi
ambo le corti del ciel manifeste.
O isplendor di Dio, per cu'io vidi
l'alto triunfo del regno verace,
dammi virtù a dir com'io il vidi!

53. *Par.* XXXIII, 55:

Da quinci innanzi il mio veder fu maggio
che 'l parlar nostro, ch'a tal vista cede,
e cede la memoria a tanto oltraggio.
Qual è colui che somniando vede,
che dopo il sogno la passione impressa
rimane, a l'altro alla mente non riede,
cotal son io, chè quasi tutta cessa
mia visione, ed ancor me distilla
nel core il dolce che nacque da essa.

54. St. Augustine, *Confessions*, trans. William Watts (2 v.; London, 1913), VII, 17: Et pervenit ad id, quod est, in ictu trepidantis aspectus tunc vero invisibilia tua per ea quae facta sunt intellecta conspexi, sed

aciem figere non evalui, et repercussa infirmitate redditus solitis, non me-
cum ferebam nisi amantem memoriam et quasi olefacta desiderantem,
quae comedere nondum possem.

55. John Burnaby, *Amor Dei* (London, 1938), 155–156, 33 ff. This is
a study of St. Augustine's teaching on the love of God and the motive
of the Christian life.

56. *Par.* XXXIII, 76:

> Io credo, per l'acume ch'io soffersi
>   del vivo raggio, ch'i'sarei smarrito,
>   se li occhi miei da lui fossero aversi.
> E mi ridorda ch'io fui più ardito
>   per questo a sostener, tanto ch'i'giunsi
>   l'aspetto mio col valore infinito.

57. *Par.* XXXIII, 82:

> O abbondante grazia ond'io presunsi
>   ficcar lo viso per la luce etterna,
>   tanto che la veduta vi consunsi!
> Nel suo profondo vidi che s'interna,
>   legato con amore in un volume,
>   ciò che per l'universo si squaderna:
> sustanze e accidenti e lor costume,
>   quasi conflati insieme, per tal modo
>   che ciò ch'i'dico è un semplice lume.
> La forma universal di questo nodo
>   credo ch'l'vidi, perchè più di largo,
>   dicendo questo, mi sento ch'i'godo.

58. *Par.* XXXIII, 100:

> A quella luce cotal si diventa,
>   che volgersi de lei per altro aspetto
>   è impossibil che mai si consenta;
> però che 'l ben, ch'è del volere obietto,
>   tutto s'accoglie in lei, e fuor di quella
>   è defettivo ciò ch'è lì perfetto.

Dante here has a sight of God as the perfect Good, the word *aspetto*
or sight used as the object of the sense, whereas in line 81 it is used
to mean the sense itself. On God's essence as supreme being and supreme good see the classic discussion by Etienne Gilson, *The Spirit of
Medieval Philosophy*, trans. A. H. C. Downes (New York, 1940),
42 ff.

Notes to V: "Eros" and "Amore"

59. *Par.* XXXIII, 137:

> Veder volea come si convenne
> l'imago al cerchio e come vi s'indova;
> ma non eran da ciò le proprie penne:
> se non che la mia mente fu percossa
> da un fulgore in che sua voglia venne.
> All'alta fantasia qui mancò possa;
> ma già volgeva il mio disio e 'l velle,
> sì come rota ch'igualmente è mossa,
> l'amor che move il sole e l'altre stelle.

60. Paget Toynbee in his edition of Dante's letters cites (191) a passage from the *Benjamin major* IV, 23 (*P.L.*, 196: col. 167B-C), on the impossibility of remembering what one has seen in a supernatural rapture and, paradoxically, remembering that one has seen far more than can actually be recalled. The relevant part reads: Et quamvis inde aliquid in memoria teneamus, et quasi per medium velum et velut in medio nebulae videamus, nec modum quidem videndi, nec qualitatem visionis comprehendere, vel recordari sufficimus. Et mirum in modum reminiscentes non reminiscimur, et non reminiscentes reminiscimur, dum videntes non pervidemus, et aspicientes non perspicimus, et intendentes non penetramus.

61. See, for example, the stimulating essay of Bruno Nardi, "Dante profeta," in *Dante e la cultura medievale*, 336 ff. Nardi discusses Dante's synthesis of kinds of prophetic vision and dreams and also takes the poet's claims to prophetic inspiration seriously. Although he rightly plays down the importance of the apocryphal *Visio sancti Pauli* except to say that it enjoyed considerable prestige, he does nothing with the Pauline tradition of kinds of visions or with the force of Dante's identification with St. Paul in the light of the long tradition of controversy about the apostle's experience.

V: Plato's "Eros" and Dante's "Amore"

1. See the study by J. A. Symonds, "The Dantesque and Platonic Ideals of Love," in *The Key of Blue and Other Prose Essays* (London, 1893), 55–86. Symonds is not clear concerning the speculative and moral attitude both Dante and Plato assumed in regard to their respective love traditions. Neither Dante nor Plato ignored the social context in which Eros and "amore" were imbedded, but both emphasized the metaphysical and personal aspects of love. On the sources of

Notes to V: "Eros" and "Amore"

Dante's platonism and on medieval platonism in general much work remains to be done. Yet, questions of sources aside, human experience, moral, imaginative, and intellectual, repeats itself, not without difference to be sure, but still in broad outline the same. The recurrence of similar experiences and values leads to their formulation in similar conceptual terms. Both thought and imagination have their own internal rules of development, and similar experiences will express themselves in similar concepts and images as both faculties elaborate their data in the attempt to render them intelligible.

2. Nardi pointed out how the *Vita nuova* and *Comedy* stand in a relationship to Provençal and *stil nuovo* speculations and representations of love similar to that of the *Phaedrus* and *Symposium* to Greek traditions. The history of the Italian lyric up to Dante seems to recapitulate the stages of development which culminated in the conception of Eros presented by Socrates in those two dialogues. Nardi traces a development of love from Andreas through Cavalcanti and Guinizelli who conclude that the beauty of the beloved comes from heaven and is destined to return there and that this beauty arouses in the gentle heart every noble virtue by means of love. Such was the doctrine as Dante received it. He added a new theme, that of the death of the beloved. In dying, she became a "spiral bellezza grande" (*Vita nuova* XXXIII, 8), and it is from this death that the platonism and mysticism of Dante arises. This is the doctrine of both the *Vita nuova* and the *Comedy*. Concerning the *Convivio*, Nardi maintains that the substance of the doctrine of love in that unfinished work is the same—with the exception of the significance of Beatrice—as that of the *Comedy* although the astrological and physiological determinism of the *Convivio* is overcome in the *Comedy* (Bruno Nardi, *Dante e la cultura medievale*, ch. i). Thus in *Convivio* II, viii, 4-5, the influence of Venus is held to be the cause of love, although this influence cannot act on or through the dead. Therefore, Dante has a second love after Beatrice. But in the *Purgatorio*, Dante accepts full responsibility for the "second love." Nardi attributes this harmony between the *Vita nuova* and the *Comedy* to a second draft of the former work, the work we now possess having been rewritten after the abandonment of the *Convivio*. Nardi gives a purely allegorical interpretation of the "lady philosophy" without, however, attempting to account for the fact that the *donna gentile* is the occasion for an analysis of physical

human beauty as well as the beauty of wisdom (Nardi, *Nel mondo di Dante*, chs. i and ii).

3. The following editions and translations of the *Phaedrus* and *Symposium* have been especially useful: R. Hackforth, *Plato's Phaedrus*, trans. with introduction and commentary (Cambridge, Eng., 1952); *The Symposium of Plato*, ed. with introduction, critical notes, and commentary by R. G. Bury (2d ed.; Cambridge, 1932); also the texts and translations in the *Phaedrus* by H. N. Fowler (London, 1944) and the *Symposium* by W. R. M. Lamb (London, 1925).

4. Hackforth, *op. cit.*, 94.

5. *Ibid.*, 57, 62, 81–84. In both the *Phaedrus* and the *Symposium* Plato tends to emphasize ideal Eros as it manifests itself in philosophical lovers, but he does give attention to the "followers of Ares," to love as an ennobling passion which produces martial and civic virtue. Analogously, in the fourth book of the *Convivio*, Dante considers love as productive of *nobilitade*, the virtues and dispositions of the soul which make a true gentleman, and tells how they are acquired through divine grace and philosophy.

6. F. M. Cornford, *Plato's Cosmology*, the *Timaeus* of Plato (London, 1937), 156.

7. *Ibid.*, 356.

8. In Dante, the relationship which exists between the power and capacity of sublimated erotic experience and the striving after values is implicit already in "Amor e 'l cor gentil sono una cosa." *Gentil cor* is the subject of both sublimated sexual love and striving for spiritual value. "Amore" actuates the "noble soul," and the fruits of this activity are the virtues. Cf. *Conv.* IV, xx.

9. On the question of the value and status of personal beauty in the Middle Ages see De Bruyne, *Etudes d'esthétique médiévale*, II, 173–202, esp. 199–200.

10. See the translation and commentary of F. M. Cornford, *The Republic of Plato* (Oxford, 1941), 66–68, 74–75.

11. *Pur.* XV, 115:

> Quando l'anima mia tornò di fori
> all cose che son fuor di lei vere,
> io riconobbi i miei non falsi errori.

12. *De monarchia* III, 4, 51 ff.: Dicit Augustinus in Civitate Dei: "Non omnia quae gesta narrantur etiam significare aliquid putanda

sunt; sed propter illa quae aliquid significant, etiam ea quae nihil significant, attexuntur. Solo vomere terra proscinditur; sed ut hoc fieri possit, etiam caetera aratri membra sunt necessaria."

13. J. D. Sinclair, *The Divine Comedy*, I, 70.

14. *Pur.* XVII, 13:

> O immaginativa che ne rube
> tal volta sì di fuor, ch'om non s'accorge
> perchè dintorno suonin mille tube,
> che move te, se 'l senso non ti porge?
> Moveti lume che nel ciel s'informa,
> per sè o per voler che giù lo scorge.

Cf. *Par.* III, 52:

> Li nostri affetti che solo infiammati
> son nel piacer dello Spirito Santo,
> letizian del suo ordine formati.

15. *Pur.* XXIV, 49:

> Ma dì s'i'veggio qui colui che fore
> trasse le nove rime, cominciando
> *"Donne ch'avete intelletto d'amore."*
> E io a lui: "I'mi son un che, quando
> Amor mi spira, noto, e a quel modo
> ch'e' ditta dentro vo significando."

16. *De vulgari eloquentia* II, iv, 69 ff.: Sed cautionem atque discretionem hanc accipere, sicut decet, hoc opus et labor est; quoniam nunquam sine strenuitate ingenii et artis assiduitate scientiarumque habitu fieri potest. Et ii sunt quos poeta Aeneidorum sexto Dei dilectos et ardente virtute sublimatos ad aethera deorumque filios vocat, quamquam figurate loquatur.

For poets whose writings have given them authority as teachers see *ibid.* I, ix, 17–21; x, 25; xii, 10, 45; II, v, 24. On the divine gift of poetry invoked from the muses, Apollo, or the constellations see *Inf.* II, 7; XXXII, 10; *Pur.* I, 8; XXII, 105; XXIX, 37–42; *Par.* I, 13–27; XVIII, 82; XXII, 121; *Ep.* X, sec. 45; *Ecloga* I, 54.

17. *Ep.* X, 18, 304 ff.: Rhetores enim consuevere praelibere dicenda, ut animum comparent auditoris. Sed poetae non solum hoc faciunt, quinimmo post haec invocationem quandam emittunt. Et hoc est eis conveniens, quia multa invocatione opus est eis, quum aliquid contra communem modum hominum a superioribus substantiis petendum sit, quasi divinum quoddam munus.

18. Natural love, Eros, or the upward movement is a cosmological and universal principle. Its impulse is naturally right. The love of the mind, of a free creature, is liable to error, however. *Pur.* XVII, 91:

> "Nè creator nè creatura mai,"
> cominciò el "figliuol, fu sanza amore,
> o naturale o d'animo e tu 'l sai.
> Lo naturale è sempre sanza errore,
>   ma l'altro puote errar per malo obietto
>   o per troppo o per poco di vigore."

" 'Neither Creator nor creature, my son, was ever without love, either natural or of the mind,' he began 'and this thou knowest; the natural is always without error, but the other may err through a wrong object or through excess or defect of vigor.' "

The distinction between true and false loves and the possibility of diverting natural love from its true course arises in the rational order. Eros, so to speak, may err. But it is guided, not only by reason, but by grace which is the power by which true love is kindled and ordered. *Par.* X, 82:

> "Quando
> lo raggio della grazia, onde s'accende
> verace amore e che poi cresce amando,
> multiplicato in te tanto resplende,
>   che ti conduce su per quella scala
>   u'sanza risalir nessun discende;
> qual ti negasse il vin della sua fiala
>   per la tua sete, in libertà non fora
>   se non com'acqua ch'al mar non si cala."

" 'Since the beam of grace by which true love is kindled and which then grows by loving shines so multiplied in thee that it brings thee up that stair which none descends but to mount again, he that should refuse to thy thirst the wine from his vessel would be no more at liberty than water that does not fall to the sea.' "

Cf. also *Par.* I, 136 ff., and *Par.* IV, 124 ff.

19. There are some other interesting references and resemblances to Plato in the works of Dante. In the *Vita nuova* (XII), Love appears in a vision as a curious mixture of youth and age, an image which recalls the *Symposium* where Eros is presented as both the youngest and the oldest of the gods. Dante was also platonic in his doctrine of creation which is a more or less "Christianized" version of the *Timaeus.*

God immediately and directly created the incorruptible things: (a) angels, (b) matter, (c) heaven, (d) the intellectual soul of man. The intelligences and their spheres created mutable, contingent things through their efficacy according to divine eternal archetypes. Given God and what he immediately creates, the rest of the process of creation is *Timaeus* doctrine with its three elements: (a) divine archetypes, (b) middle causes corresponding to the Demiurge, (c) an unformed matter which they "inform." See *Conv.* III, xiv, 2–8; *Par.* VII, 64–75, 124–144; XIII, 52–66; XXIX, 13–18, 28–36; *De mon.* II, 2, 15–38. For angels as middle causes see *Par.* XIII, 61–66. Gerhardt Ledig in his article "Dante als Platoniker" (*Jahrbuch der Dante Gesellschaft* [XXVI; Leipzig, 1946]) points out some interesting similarities between Dante and Plato as persons, in their political attitudes and in their manner of reaction to temporal events. Both of them shared an intense political interest, and both were "failures" in political life. They set against the confusion of temporal reality a supersensory "beyond" conceived in richly symbolic and mythic terms (138–139).

20. This idea is a medieval commonplace. A classic statement is Boethius' in the *Consolatio philosophiae* III, metrum 9, 18–25.

21. The striking similarities between Plato and Dante were observed by some of the Renaissance humanists and critics. Ficino and Landino interpreted the *Comedy* as a platonic work, and Mazzoni praises Dante as having given the world a representation of the intelligible world itself. Mazzoni expressly refers to the *Phaedrus* (247) in which Plato denies the possibility of describing the world above the heavens and says that Plato would have had to acknowledge his error if he had been able to read the *Paradiso* (Introduction to Mazzoni's *Della difesa della "Commedia" di Dante*). As the Renaissance platonists never tired of emphasizing, inspiration is really a kind of recollection of the real or intelligible world which is the true dwelling place of the soul. The poet, in their view, remembers more of this world above than less gifted mortals, and he can find images and symbols for expressing at least a part of that essentially inexpressible reality. To find some mode of expression which will suggest the quality and content of his transcendent vision requires learning and training, and, since true poetry is of this kind and presupposes an essentially supernatural experience, he will employ allegory, for allegory is the mode for expressing depth of meaning. The poet will also be a lover who will understand how love awakens by an external visible beauty which

activates an internal reminiscence of a supernatural beauty. It is evident how Dante met all the Renaissance criteria for the true poet. Cf. Raffaele Resta, *Dante e la filosofia d'amore* (Bologna, 1935), 141-166.

22. *Par.* XXX, 56.

23. *Pur.* XVI, 85.

24. Symonds, "The Dantesque and Platonic Ideals of Love." Symonds' essay is written entirely from the point of view of the abnormality of "amore" and Eros.

25. Edward Moore, *Studies in Dante* (3d ser.; Oxford, 1903), 221-252; Charles Williams, *The Figure of Beatrice* (London, 1943); Etienne Gilson, *Dante et la philosophie* (Paris, 1939), especially the first chapter.

VI: Dante's Sun Symbolism and the Visions of the Blessed

1. Baeumker, *Witelo*, 356 ff.

2. See also De Bruyne, *Etudes d'esthétique médiévale*, III, 17 ff.

3. Baeumker, *op. cit.*, 362 ff.

4. *Ibid.*, 362-372. Baeumker gives many examples of the use of this metaphor in the Middle Ages. See, for example, St. Augustine's *Soliloquia* I, 8, 15; *P.L.*, 32: col. 877: Ergo quo modo in hoc sole tria quaedam licet animadverter, quod est quod fulget, quod illuminat: ita in illo secretissimo Deo, quem vis intelligere, tria quaedam sunt, quod est, quod intelligitur et quod cetera facit intelligi.

5. *Pur.* VII, 25:

> Non per far, ma per non fare, ho perduto
> a veder l'alto sol che tu disiri
> e che fu tardi per me conosciuto.

6. *Par.* IX, 7:

> E già la vita di quel lume santo
> rivolta s'era al Sol che la riempie
> come quel ben ch'a ogni cosa è tanto.

7. *Par.* X, 52:

> Ringrazia,
> ringrazia il sol delli angeli, ch'a questo
> sensibil t'ha levato per sua grazia.

8. *Par.* XVIII, 100:

> Poi come nel percuoter de'ciocchi arsi
> surgono innumerabili faville,
> onde li stolti sogliono augurarsi;

> resurger parver quindi più di mille
> luci, e salir, qual assai e qual poco
> sì come il sol che l'accende sortille;

9. *Par.* XXV, 52:

> "La Chiesa militante alcun figliuolo
> non ha con più speranza, com'è scritto
> nel sol che raggia tutto nostro stuolo."

Cf. *Par.* XVIII, 64 ff.: God as the source of all light in the mode of grace and understanding.

10. *Par.* XXX, 124:

> Nel giallo della rosa sempiterna,
> che si dilata ed ingrada e redole
> odor di lode al sol che sempre verna,
> qual è colui che tace e dicer vole,
> mi trasse Beatrice.

11. *Par.* X, 76:

> Poi, sì cantando, quelli ardenti soli
> si fuor girati intorno a noi tre volte,
> come stelle vicine a' fermi poli,
> donne mi parver non da ballo sciolte,
> ma che s'arrestin tacite, ascoltando
> fin che le nove note hanno ricolte.

12. *Pur.* XVI, 106:

> Soleva Roma, che 'l buon mondo feo,
> due soli aver, che l'una e l'altra strada
> facean vedere, e del mondo e di Deo.

13. *De monarchia* III, 1, 34 ff.; 4, 10 ff. Cf. also *Ep.* VIII, 141 ff., where Rome is described as bereft of her two luminaries. The image of two suns is an unusual one. Bruno Nardi (*Nel mondo di Dante,* 158) suggests a possible source in the treatment of the phenomenon of parhelion in Albertus Magnus. Kantorowicz, however, suggests a source in the Byzantine tradition of symbolizing both the Emperor and Christ as suns (Ernst H. Kantorowicz, "Dante's 'Two Suns,'" *Semitic and Oriental Studies,* Univ. of California Publ. in Semitic Philology, XI [1951], 217–231).

14. *Par.* XI, 50: "nacque al mondo un sole." Cf. *Inf.* XVI for the passage on which the claim that Dante intended to become, or actually became, a Franciscan is based. The cord which he removes and gives to Virgil and which Virgil casts into the darkness as a signal is, on this

hypothesis, the Franciscan girdle. See *La Divina Commedia di Dante Alighieri*, ed. and annotated by C. H. Grandgent (Boston, 1933), 143–144, for a brief discussion of this matter and appropriate bibliographical references.

15. *Inf.* XI, 91:

> "O sol che sani ogni vista turbata,
> tu mi contenti sì quando tu solvi,
> che, non men che saver, dubbiar m'aggrata."

16. *Par.* XXX, 75: "il sol delli occhi miei"; *Par.* III, 1: "Quel sol che pria mi scaldò 'l petto."

17. *Pur.* VI, 43:

> Veramente a così alto sospetto
> non ti fermar, se quella nol ti dice
> che lume fia tra 'l vero lo 'ntelletto:
> non so se 'ntendi; io dico di Beatrice.

18. The image of God as the sun of justice is frequent in medieval literature and its source is biblical, Mal. 4: 1.

19. *Pur.* XIII, 16:

> "O dolce lume a cui fidanza i'entro
> per lo novo cammin, tu ne conduci"
> dicea "come condur si vuol quinc'entro.
> Tu scaldi il mondo, tu sovr'esso luci:
> s'altra ragione in contrario non pronta,
> esser dien sempre li tuoi raggi duci."

20. *Pur.* VII, 22:

> "Per tutt'i cerchi del solente regno"
> rispuosi lui "son io di qua venuto:
> virtù del ciel mi mossi, e con lei vegno.
> Non per far, ma per non fare ho perduto
> a veder l'alto sol che tu disiri
> e che fu tardi per me conosciuto."

21. *Pur.* VII, 28: "Luogo è là giù non tristo da martiri, / ma di tenebre solo.

22. *Pur.* XXII, 61: "Se così è, qual sole o qual candele / ti stenebraron."

23. *Pur.* IV, 62: "Quello specchio / che su e giù del suo lume conduce.

24. *Par.* XX, 1:

> Quando colui che tutto 'l mondo alluma

dell'emisperio nostro sì discende,
che 'l giorno d'ogne parte si consuma,
lo ciel, che sol di lui prima s'accende,
subitamente si rifà parvente
per molte luci, in che una risplende;
e questo atto del ciel mi venne a mente,
come 'l segno del mondo e de' suoi duci
nel benedetto rostro fu tacente;
però che tutte quelle vive luci,
vie più lucendo, cominciaron canti
da mia memoria labili e caduci.
O dolce amor che di riso t'ammanti,
quanto parevi ardente in que' flailli,
ch'avìeno spirto sol di pensier santi!

25. *Par.* XXIII, 25:

Quale ne' plenilunii sereni
Trivia ride tra le ninfe etterne
che dipingon lo ciel per tutti i seni,
vidi sopra miglaiia di lucerne
un sol che tutte quante l'accendea,
come fa il nostro le viste superne;
e per la viva luce trasperea
la lucente sustanza tanto chiara
nel viso mio, che non la sostenea.

26. *Par.* XXIII, 70:

"Perchè la faccia mia sì t'innamora,
che non ti rivolgi al bel giardino
che sotto i raggi di Cristo s'infiora?"

27. *Par.* XXIII, 79:

Come a raggio di sol che puro mei
per fratta nube già prato di fiori
vider, coverti d'ombra, li occhi miei;
vid'io così più turbe di splendori,
fulgorate di su da raggi ardenti,
sanza veder principio di fulgori.

Cf. Rev. 21: 22 for Christ as sun of the New Universe.

28. *Par.* XXXII, 106:

Così ricorsi ancora alla dottrina

Notes to VI: Sun Symbolism

di colui ch'abbelliva di Maria
come del sole stella mattutina.

29. *Par.* XXI, 37–42:

Poi altre vanno via sanza ritorno,
altre rivolgon sè onde son mosse,
e altre roteando fan soggiorno;
tal modo parve me che quivi fosse
in quello sfavillar che 'nsieme venne,
sì come in certo grado si percosse.

30. On the astrological background of the visual and physical characteristics of the planets as well as the astrological appropriateness of the imagery Dante employs in the various planets (e.g., water or fish in the "moist" planets, the moon and Mercury, daws in Saturn, etc.) see Rudolf Palgen, *Dantes Sternglaube, Beiträge zur Erklärung des Paradiso* (Heidelberg, 1940). On the angelological correspondences to the souls and their spheres see Edmund Gardner, *Dante's Ten Heavens* (Westminster, 1898), 22 ff., and Antonio Lubin's commentary *La Commedia di Dante Alighieri* (Padua, 1881). Irma Brandeis has acutely analyzed the variety of Dante's metaphors and related each kind to the different realities the poet is describing in each of the three parts and to the awareness of the pilgrim at different stages of the journey ("Metaphor in the *Divine Comedy*," *Hudson Review*, VIII [1956], 557–575). On the number of similes in the various sections of the *Comedy* see H. F. Tozer, *Dante, La Divina Commedia: English Commentary* (Oxford, 1901), 404; on the Mansions of Beatitude see Gardner, *op. cit.*, 12 ff.

31. Gardner, *op. cit.*, 107–109.

32. *Par.* XIV, 109–118.

33. There is the problem whether we are to assume that the souls in Mars or Jupiter are necessarily more beatified than, for example, SS. Thomas and Bonaventura in the sphere of the Sun. Gardner suggests (*op. cit.*, 111) that "most probably Dante would have us understand in general that this sphere of Mars represents a higher grade of perfection as indicated by the greater beauty of this sphere and of its souls without necessarily supposing that any special spirit in the sun is enjoying a less perfect vision than one in this or another higher sphere, since there are clearly degrees in each."

34. Dante's *Paradiso* is, of course, made up of *specula* insofar as

all the things in it reflect the divine light in some degree. The angels reflect it like mirrors (XIII, 94), the soul is a mirror (*specchio*, XVIII, 2), and God himself is like a mirror (*speglio*, XV, 62; XXVI, 106) although he is the source of light.

35. Cf. Gardner, *op. cit.*, 141, 130–136.

36. *Par.* XXIII, 79–84:

> Come a raggio di sol che puro mei
> per fratta nube già prato di fiori
> vider, coverti d'ombra, li occhi miei;
> vid'io così più turbe di splendori,
> fulgorate di su da raggi ardenti,
> sanza veder principio di fulgori.

37. God is rendered as light both as Trinity and as Unity. The Second Person is a living light (*viva luce*) radiating from the Father as from a source (*lucente*) and bound to him by the Third Person, Love. The living light, although one with the other persons of the Trinity refracts itself into the lights of the celestial hierarchy, yet remaining one in itself, and descends by degrees to make the whole splendor of the creation (*Par.* XIII, 52–81). Creation in turn receives the divine light according to the fitness of its parts (XXXI, 22). Similarly, at the final vision, the Son appeared to Dante as a reflected light, derived from a source, yet also the source itself (XXXIII, 27–28). As Unity, God is the true light (*verace luce*, III, 32) and the highest light whose beams are eternal (XXXII, 71; XXXI, 72). In XXXIII alone we find the following references to God as light: *Eterno Lume* (43); *Alta Luce* (54); *Somma Luce* (64); *Vivo Raggio* (77); *Luce Eterna* (83); *Luce* (100); *Vivo Lume* (100); *Alto Lume* (116); *Luce Eterna* (124). Note how the same light vocabulary is applied to God, angels, and souls.

Index

Index

Angelic Lady, 66, 81-83
Angels, as light, 12, 164
Appetition, 63-65
Apprehension, 63-65
Augustine, St., 11, 98-99
  on beauty, 68-75, 173 n.32
  on forms of vision, 89
  on ladder of beauty, 193 n.42
  on love, 51
  as mystic, 100
  sun symbolism of, 143-144
  on vision of God, 87-90
Autobiography, spiritual, 33-34

Beatrice, 103, 107, 113, 128, 132, 144, 153
  and *donna gentile*, 119-120
  and *donna pietosa*, 118
  as guide, 121, 139
  and Holy Spirit, 3
  interpretations of, 139
  and lady philosophy, 113-114, 119-120
  as mediator, 10
  role of, 133
  self-definition of, 20-21
  as sun, 146-147
Beauty, 18-20, 75-78, 173 n.32
  of body, 19, 67, 116
  as divine lure, 73, 138
  feminine, medieval ideal of, 79
  form as, 75-76
  light as, 81-82
  and love, 14
  medieval speculation on, 67-68
  of person, 80-81, 116, 136-137
  primacy of, 122, 124, 138
  similitude and correspondence as, 71-72, 77, 192 n.35
Beloved, role of, in Dante and Plato, 132, 135, 139-140
Benjamin major (De contempla-tione), 98-99
Benvenuto Da Imola, 157
Bernard, St., 98-99, 107, 134
  on beauty of person, 80-81

  as mystic, 100
  on rapture, 91-92
  on vision of God, 90-92
Boethius, 187-188 n.17
  on love, 51-52
Bonagiunta da Lucca, 7-8, 130
Bonaventura, St., on beauty, 76-78

Cacciaguida, 102, 159
  see also Anchises-Cacciaguida ty-pology
Chanson de Roland, 79-80
Christ, 102, 160
  as sun, 148-149, 160, 163
  see also Adam-Christ typology
Church Militant, 160
Church Triumphant, 160
City of God, 69
Coaptation, 64-65
Complacentia, 64-65, 189 n.23
Confessions, 73
Connaturality, 63
Consideration, kinds of, 3-4, 91-92, 197 n.20
Contemplation, 4-5, 91-97, 197 n.20
  Dante vs. St. Thomas on, 96
  kinds of, 3-4
Convivio, 26-27, 31, 41, 120-121, 128
  beauty in, 81-83
  love in, 52-57, 114-117
  philosophy in, 117-118
Corinthians, First Epistle to the, 85
Corinthians, Second Epistle to the, 84-85, 88, 98, 104
Cross, symbolism of, 158-159

Dante, 5, 113
  his confession in *Purgatorio*, 20-21, 120
  his recollection of mystical ex-perience, 57-58
  as Renaissance poet, 208-209 n.21
  see also Paul (St.)-Dante typol-ogy *and* Aeneas-Dante typol-ogy
Death, of love, 21
De consideratione, 98-99

216

Index

Index

Mirror(s), 4, 114
    created universe as divine, 4, 86
    see also *Speculum*
Modus-species-ordo, 75
Moses-St.Paul typology, 86-89, 93-94,
    102
Myth, 42, 129

Natural place, doctrine of, 50-52
Novella vista, 5, 106
    see also Sight, new sense of

Paradiso:
    brightness in, role of, 16, 161-162
    chain of prayer in, 5, 133
    circular causation in, 16-18
    final image-sequence in, 48, 165
    final visions in, 106-110, 166
    imagery of, 151-152
    light in, role of, 14-18
    as lyrical pageant, 151
    modes of vision of, and structure,
        104
    natural and supernatural journeys
        in, 4-5, 168-169 n.3
    process of ascent in, 17
Paul, St., 4
    Dante's self-identification with,
        98-103
    as mystic:
        Dante on, 97-106
        theological debate on, 85-97
        mystical experience of, 84-85
    see also Aeneas-St.Paul typology
        and Moses-St. Paul typology
Paul(St.)-Dante typology, 98-103
Personality, Dante's emphasis on, 132
Phaedrus, 2, 18-20, 121-124, 127, 131
    neoplatonic interpretation of, 173-
        175 n.33
Philosophy:
    beauty of, 117-118
    and love, 117
Piacere, 65
    see also *Complacentia*
Plain of truth, 7, 20, 57, 124, 134

Platonism, medieval, 2, 167 n.1
Plotinus, 90
    on beauty, 68
    on light, 78
Poet, 8
    Christian, 40
    as imitative artist, 123, 128-130
        inspired, 123, 128
    as prophet, 40, 131, 181 n.21
    as rival:
        of philosopher, 39, 131
        of philosopher, theologian, and
            prophet, 45-46
    see also Lover-poet
Poetry:
    Dante's revaluation of, 8-9
    as dictation of love, 7
    divine gift of, 129
    inspired, 7, 128-130
    scholastic and patristic attacks on,
        8
    and truth, 8, 129
Poet-theologian, 40
Pope, as sun, 145-146
Porphyry, 90, 190 n.26
Prophecy, kinds of, 93-94
Pseudo-Dionysius the Areopagite,
    see Dionysius
Purgatorio, 57-59, 61-63

Rapture, 91-92, 94-97
    controversy on St. Paul's, 81-97
        passim
Republic, 10-11, 142-143
Res and *signa*, 30, 37
Richard of St. Victor, 98-99
    on contemplation and rapture, 91-
        93
    as mystic, 100
    on vision of God, 91-93
Romans, Epistle to the, 85-86, 95
Rose, eternal:
    transformations of, 48
    vision of, 3

Saints, as suns, 145

219

Index